The United
States
in the Indian
Wars

The United States in the Indian Wars

Don Lawson

Illustrated with
photographs, and maps and drawings
by Robert F. McCullough

Abelard-Schuman
New York

Library of Congress Cataloging in Publication Data
Lawson, Don.
    The United States in the Indian wars.

    (The Young People's history of America's wars series.)
Bibliography: p. Includes index.
    SUMMARY: A survey of the causes, events and aftermath of
the numerous wars between the Indians and the white settlers
from 1637 to 1890. 1. Indians of North America—Wars—Juve-
nile literature. [1. Indians of North America—Wars.]   I.
McCullough, Robert F., 1929–   II. Title.
E81.L35 1975   973   75–6684
ISBN 0–200–00158–2

Manufactured in the United States of America

10 9 8 7 6 5 4 3 2 1

Contents

Illustrations

Time Line

1637
Pequot Indian War in New England.

1675–1676
King Philip's Indian War in New England.

1689–1763
Colonial Wars in America.
King William's War (1689–1697)
Queen Anne's War (1702–1713)
King George's War (1744–1748)
French and Indian War (1754–1763)

1763
Pontiac's conspiracy.

1775–1783
American Revolution.

1794
Battle of Fallen Timbers—Rise of Tecumseh.

1811

Battle of Tippecanoe—Defeat of Tecumseh's
brother, the Shawnee Prophet.

1812–1816

War of 1812.

1830

Passage of Indian Removal Bill and
creation of Indian Territory.

1835–1842

Seminole Indian War.

1860

Pony Express begins; invention
of Spencer repeating rifle.

1861

Telegraph line completed between St. Louis and
San Francisco; Gatling gun patented.

1861–1865

American Civil War.

1862

Uprising of Santee Sioux in Minnesota.

1863–1864

Kit Carson's campaigns against the Navajos and
Apaches in southwest.

1864

Sand Creek Massacre.

1866

Fetterman Massacre.

1867
Invention of dynamite by Alfred Nobel.

1869
Union Pacific and Central Pacific
transcontinental railroad completed.

1870
Construction started on Northern Pacific railroad.

1872–1873
Modoc Indian War; Yellowstone
National Park established.

1874–1875
Red River Indian War.

1876
Custer's Last Stand.

1877
Flight of the Nez Percés.

1879
Ute Indian War.

1885
Extermination of last great buffalo herd.

1886
Geronimo surrenders.

1889–1890
Wovoka starts Ghost Dance religious movement.

1890
Sitting Bull slain; Wounded Knee massacre.

1
The
Fetterman Massacre

"Give me eighty men, and I'll conquer the whole Sioux nation."

Those were the arrogant words spoken by Captain William J. Fetterman, United States cavalry officer stationed at Wyoming's newly built Fort Phil Kearny, on a winter's day in 1866. Captain Fetterman was to get his eighty men, but he was to lead them not to victory over the Sioux but to disaster.

It was less than a week before Christmas and Colonel Henry B. Carrington, Fort Kearny's commanding officer, had ordered a large supply of wood to be brought into the fort from a nearby pine forest. In addition to tree trunks for fuel, several of the soldiers who had wives and families with them at Fort Perilous or Fort Disaster, as they had nicknamed their post, planned on returning with small pine trees to decorate for Christmas.

Although the stand of timber was only half a dozen miles away, it was a dangerous journey in the slow-moving, mule-drawn wagons. Fort Kearny had been under a state of siege for several months with Indian Chief Red Cloud and his Sioux, Arapahoe and Cheyenne warriors killing outright or capturing and torturing to death anyone who ventured, unprotected, outside the fortress walls.

On this particular morning—December 21, 1866—the wood train had safely reached the forest. Now, loaded with logs and Christmas trees, it was just starting its return journey when a lookout high atop Fort Kearny's walls shouted, "Indians are attacking the wood train!"

Colonel Carrington had kept a cavalry detachment on the alert, and he immediately gave them orders to mount and ride. As the men dashed to their horses the cavalry trumpet call, "Boots and Saddles," sounded

The Morning Drill
PHOTO: COLUMBIA JOURNALISM REVIEW

within the fortress walls and echoed through the surrounding hills. The Indians now knew exactly what was coming next, but they were more than ready for the approaching cavalry attack.

As a matter of fact, the Indians' attack on the wood train had been a carefully planned ruse, a trick to lure a force of cavalry outside the fort, where it could be ambushed and destroyed. The red men had many old scores to settle with the white men. Two years earlier, almost to the day, white soldiers had made a surprise attack on an Indian village at Sand Creek when most of the braves were away hunting. More than 125 Indians—three-quarters of them women and children —had been killed, scalped and otherwise mutilated. And in recent months the white men had broken yet one more treaty with the red men by invading Indian Territory and building forts such as Fort Kearny along the Bozeman Trail. The time had come, a war council had decided, to drive the white men out of Indian Territory once and for all.

The man who insisted upon leading the party to rescue the wood train was Captain Fetterman, and under his command were those eighty men he had boastfully requested a short time before. His two officer aides were Captain Frederick H. Brown—who had boasted that he would take Sioux Chief Red Cloud's scalp—and Lieutenant George W. Grummond, a newlywed whose bride was one of the two dozen women and children inside Fort Kearny.

As Captain Fetterman swung astride his horse, Colonel Carrington reminded him that his orders were to rescue the wood train. "You are not, repeat not, to pursue the Indians if they retreat. And that's a direct order!"

"Yes, *sir!*" Captain Fetterman snapped, and spurred his horse through the open main gate. His command followed him at a full gallop.

As soon as the Indians had attacked the wood train, the drivers of the mule teams had quickly formed their wagons into a defensive square. From behind the shelter of the wagon boxes the soldiers were now firing their single-shot Springfield rifles at the mounted warriors who circled the ambushed wagon train, pouring in their own rifle fire as well as arrows.

Captain Fetterman did not lead his troops directly toward the beleaguered wagons. Instead, he led them on a course that would take them far to the rear of the fight. His plan, observers at the fort decided, was evidently to get behind the Indians to cut off any possible retreat and then attack, driving them toward the fort.

This was exactly what the Indians had been waiting for. As Fetterman and his men advanced, they encountered small bands of additional warriors who hastily retreated. Fetterman pursued them. Soon the cavalry had ridden well past a point called Lodge Trail Ridge to another low rise, which was soon to become Massacre Ridge. Fetterman and his men did not know it, but beyond this ridge Red Cloud and another great fighting chief, Crazy Horse, lay in wait with more than 2,000 warriors.

When the Indians burst upon them with sudden,

Old Trooper and Chief
PHOTO: U.S. ARMY

mad fury, Fetterman and his command instantly knew they had been led into a trap. But it was too late now to retreat. They chose to stand and fight with the blind rage of doomed men. In a matter of moments the Indians who had been attacking the wood train abandoned that attack and galloped toward the ridge on which Fetterman and his command were fighting and dying. At this point Captain Fetterman and Captain Brown, realizing they were completely surrounded and that rescue was impossible, put pistols to their heads and committed suicide, rather than risk being captured and tortured.

But an attempt to rescue was already under way. By this time the wood train had re-formed and safely reached Fort Kearny, and Colonel Carrington had organized a relief party made up of every available man, including mule drivers, prisoners from the guardhouse, cooks, musicians from the post band and even a handful of infirmary patients. When these forty men plus the last forty able-bodied troopers and infantry that Colonel Carrington could spare were assembled, they were swiftly led to the rescue by a captain named Tenodor Ten Eyck.

The relief party, however, had at least half a dozen miles to travel, and by the time they reached Massacre Ridge every soldier in Captain Fetterman's party was dead. The Indians had lingered after killing off the last troops, taking scalps and otherwise mutilating the bodies.

When Captain Ten Eyck saw there was no chance of rescuing any of his fellow troopers, he ordered his small relief party to remain a safe distance from Massacre Ridge and the remaining Indians. As the soldiers waited they saw that a lone dog had apparently followed his master out from the fort and was now making his way about the grisly battleground searching for his master's body. As Ten Eyck and his men continued to watch, an Indian reached down to pick up the dog, perhaps to take him back to camp as a pet. But before he could reach the animal another Indian coldly fired an arrow into the dog's body, killing it. Obviously, Ten Eyck decided, the Indians intended to leave no living thing on Massacre Ridge. Sand Creek had indeed been avenged.

Ten Eyck waited until the last Indian had ridden away. Then he and his soldiers moved on to the ridge to collect their dead and carry them back to the fort.

Colonel Carrington fully expected that Red Cloud and his warriors would return that night and attack the fort. If they did, Fort Kearny would probably fall. With this in mind Colonel Carrington ordered all of the women and children at the fort into the building where gunpowder and ammunition were stored. If the fort fell, Colonel Carrington ordered one of his aides, he was to blow up the building and its occupants. Included among the occupants was Colonel Carrington's wife.

But Fort Kearny did not fall, although it was later learned that Red Cloud had indeed planned to return and attack it. The fort and its defenders were saved by a fierce blizzard that swept out of the north and sent temperatures plunging down to thirty-five degrees below zero. No one could live let alone fight in such weather.

But Colonel Carrington knew that when the storm lifted the threat from Red Cloud would once again become a reality, and there simply were not enough men within the fort to defend it successfully. Somehow, help must be summoned from Laramie. The colonel called for volunteers.

There was only one volunteer. He was a civilian scout named Portugee John Phillips. For a moment Colonel Carrington hesitated. He and Portugee John were old friends, and the colonel knew he was sending his friend to almost certain death. But he also knew there was no other choice.

"Take my horse, John. And may God ride with you." The colonel's horse was the best cavalry mount on the post, a Thoroughbred named Kentucky Red.

No one had to tell Portugee John the odds against him. He had been through other Wyoming winters, and he knew this was one of the worst storms he had faced. He also knew he must run the gantlet of Indians surrounding the fort.

But most of the Indians had been driven into their tepees by the storm. Bundled in his buffalo skin coat—inside the lining were stuffed dispatches requesting help—Portugee John rode into the teeth of the blizzard until he felt his legs growing numb. Then he dismounted and led his horse through the shoulder-deep snowdrifts. Alternating in this fashion, walking until he was ready to drop, and then remounting and

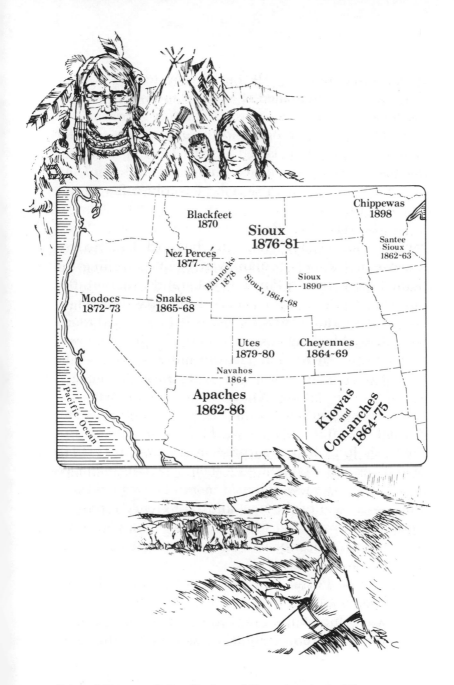

Dates of Important Indian Battles and Campaigns in the West

riding until he was all but frozen to the saddle, Portugee John managed to make it to Fort Reno late the next day. But Reno was a small fort garrisoned by only a handful of troops, and there was no means for communicating with Fort Laramie. Feeding and resting his horse and then accepting food and drink for himself, Portugee John delayed for only a few hours. Then he rode on.

Just beyond Fort Reno, the rescue mission almost came to an abrupt end. The blizzard had abated somewhat, and now Indians were again patrolling the plains. They sighted Portugee John and took out after him. He spurred the colonel's Kentucky Thoroughbred into a gallop, but some of the red men tried to cut him off by blocking his path. Portugee John spurred his mount even harder. He also unlimbered his rifle and prepared to shoot his way through the red warriors. The red men closed in on him, knowing the white scout could only fire a single shot from his Springfield, and then he would have to reload. But Portugee John had a surprise in store for them. His prized weapon—bought with money he had managed to save from the few dollars a month he was paid as a scout—was one of the new and rare Henry repeating rifles. He commenced firing at point-blank range, his shots taking a deadly toll. In a few moments he had broken into the clear.

That night Portugee John took shelter in the lee of a rocky ledge. He wanted to ride on, but he knew his horse was completely exhausted. He fed Kentucky Red first with grain from a saddlebag and cupping handfuls of snow for the animal to nibble and somewhat slake its thirst; then he ate his own supper of dry cornmeal. (The cavalryman's and scout's law was to care for one's horse first, and then look out after one's own needs.)

At dawn the horse and rider again moved out. In a few hours they reached a white settlement called Horse Shoe Station. Here there was a telegraph in working order, and Portugee John wired to Fort Laramie relaying Colonel Carrington's request for help. The telegraph operator was skeptical, however, about the message getting through, so once again the tireless scout rode on. He was offered a relief horse, but Portugee John knew no mount could match the colonel's, so the offer was refused.

Hours later—Portugee John was never afterward able to recall just how many—the horse and its semiconscious rider stumbled into Fort Laramie. The officers and their ladies at Laramie were in the midst of preparations for a pre-Christmas party when the two ice- and snow-covered figures appeared at the fort. Portugee John was helped from the saddle, and he managed to struggle to the quarters of the officer of the day.

Portugee John tried to repeat Colonel Carrington's request for aid, but he found he could not speak. Then he remembered the written orders the colonel had stuffed into the lining of his buffalo coat. He managed to pull out these dispatches, handed them to the officer of the day and then fell onto the floor, unconscious. The heroic Portugee John, carried by Colonel Carrington's faithful and equally heroic cavalry mount, had traveled almost 250 miles through one of the worst blizzards in Wyoming history.

Happily, their efforts saved Fort Kearny and its garrison—if only temporarily—and Portugee John Phillips recovered from his ordeal. Later, the United States government rewarded him with a gift of $300.

Unhappily, however, Kentucky Red did not live. The horse died from exhaustion in the snow on the Fort Laramie parade ground—but only after he had enabled his rider to successfully complete his mission.

The news of the Fetterman Massacre and Portugee John's successful rescue mission quickly traveled by telegraph to Washington and the rest of the eastern part of the country. The federal government as well as the public that was still celebrating the recent end of the Civil War suddenly awakened to the situation on the western plains. Once again, as had happened so often in the past, there was an immediate outcry against the American Indians. A major Indian uprising was obviously under way, the newspapers reported, and the murder of Captain Fetterman and his command by the red men must be avenged.

2

"Feed 'em in the Winter and Fight 'em in the Summer"

When the first Europeans came to North America they were met by the Indians, who were actually the first Americans. The red men greeted these strange white men from across the sea in friendly fashion, teaching the newcomers what crops to plant, how to build the best kinds of shelter, how and where to fish and hunt and how to find their way through the trackless wilderness—on foot in the summertime or on snowshoes in the winter. The Indians' birchbark canoes also were adopted by the white man.

For a time after the coming of the white man the Indians prospered, learning to use new tools made from iron and steel, which made agriculture easier. The Indians also prized the settlers' iron kettles and other cooking utensils. Unfortunately, the Indians also learned to use the white man's guns. At first these made hunting easier than it had been with bows and arrows, but in time the Indians learned the value of guns in warfare.

Along the eastern seaboard of America, the French and English, who soon began a life-and-death struggle for control of the North American continent, exploited the Indians' demand for weapons by debauching the red men with rum, by forms of religion that were completely foreign to the Indians' life-style and by any other available means. The Indians also fell prey to new diseases to which they were not immune. Small-pox was an especially devastating disease introduced by the white man.

The French came to North America mainly in search of furs and any other product they could take back to Europe and sell for a profit. They were not especially interested in colonization. The English, however, were interested in colonization. They wanted to settle on and own this new land. Consequently, they set about buying land from the Indians, a process that the red men failed completely to understand. Having no sense of property—no Indian could "own" land—the Indians would gladly exchange land titles for the white man's gifts, but then they would continue to hunt, fish and live on the land just as they had before it was sold. To the Indians, property titles were worth less than the paper on which they were written. To the Europeans, especially the English, property titles were sacred. With their strong sense of property rights, the English resented paying for land and not obtaining complete ownership of it. Quarrels were a natural result.

Among the most tragic of these quarrels was one between Connecticut colonists and the Pequot Indians

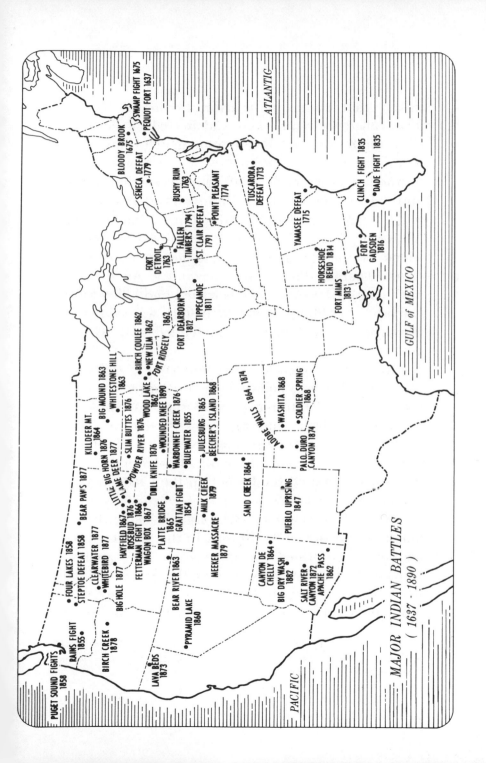

MAJOR INDIAN BATTLES
(1637 - 1890)

in 1637 that resulted in the killing of some 600 Indians. This called for retaliation, and in 1644 a Powhatan chief and his braves killed more than 300 white settlers at Jamestown.

Another tragic early conflict between the colonists and the Indians was King Philip's War, which began in 1675 and lasted until 1676. King Philip's father, Massasoit, was a Qampanoag chief, who had been a friend of the Pilgrims and had given his two sons English names, Philip and Alexander. After Massasoit's death Alexander was betrayed and killed by the English, and Philip waged a bloody war of revenge throughout New England that ended only with his death.

The French, of course, encouraged the Indians to attack the English, pointing out to the red men how the English were trying to steal their lands. As the struggle for North America grew between the French and the British, both sides tried to enlist the Indians as their allies. This competition was finally ended when the British defeated the French in the Colonial Wars, which ended in 1763.*

During the American Revolution, many Indians fought on the side of the British. In this war the British adopted the former French tactic. They told the Indians the colonists were stealing the red men's lands. For the most part, however, the Indians were not especially valuable allies of the British in the Revolu-

* For the key roles played by the Indians in America's earliest conflicts, see the first three books in this series: *The Colonial Wars*, *The American Revolution* and *The War of 1812*.

tion, although the Iroquois and the Mohawks—the latter under their leader Thayendanega, or Joseph Brant—fought with exceptional bravery. The Continental army under General John Sullivan was especially harsh in its retaliation against the Iroquois in New York State.

Even after the British were defeated in the Revolutionary War, the Indians continued to be their allies. They did so because the British seemed to be their only possible hope in preventing migrating United States settlers from overrunning all of the land west of the Appalachian Mountains. The tide of westward migration seemed relentless, although the officials of the new United States government, like the British before them, tried to make the takeover of Indian lands legitimate by buying them from the red men. When the Indians interfered with the migrating settlers, they were attacked by the United States Army, which was under orders to "protect" the settlers.

Driven to desperation, the Indians became especially staunch allies of the British in the period just prior to the War of 1812. One of the greatest of all Indian leaders, a Shawnee chief named Tecumseh, made a valiant effort to organize a number of tribes into a confederation to stem the tide of settlers. Tecumseh's effort was similar to that made earlier by Pontiac at the close of the French and Indian War, the last of the four Colonial Wars. Tecumseh's efforts proved as futile as had Pontiac's, however, when Tecumseh's combined tribes were confronted by the United States Army at Tippecanoe along the Wabash

River in Indiana. Tecumseh did not take part in this battle, but his brother, who was called the Prophet, led the Indian confederation to disastrous defeat at the hands of General William Henry Harrison. Tecumseh himself was later slain fighting alongside the British at the Battle of the Thames River during the War of 1812.

Although the young United States failed to defeat the British in the War of 1812, the fledgling nation did finally establish its complete independence. The American people now began to deal with internal national problems, the most important of which was the so-called Indian problem—a satisfactory solution to which has not been found to this day.

The first major attempt at solving the Indian problem was the passage of the Indian Removal Act of May 28, 1830. There had been other piecemeal efforts to legally move the red men out of the path of westward migration, but this was the first federally approved act that sought to solve the problem once and for all. The idea behind it was to move all Indians from east of the Mississippi River to the vast Indian Territory west of the Mississippi beyond Missouri and Arkansas. A buffer zone was to separate the red men from the white men. A part of the Indian Territory (much of which is today's Oklahoma) was also known as the Great American Desert, and it was believed no white men would ever want to live there. Nevertheless, the white men persuaded themselves that they were doing the Indians a favor in making them trade their fertile lands for semiarid wastelands because the

Indians would now have a permanent home free from interference by migrating settlers or the army.

Most of the Indian tribes resisted the Removal Act, although several tribes had already been so badly scattered that they could offer no unified resistance. The Sauk and Fox tribes, under the great chief Black Hawk, who had also fought alongside the British in the War of 1812, flatly refused to leave their lands in Illinois and Wisconsin in the Northwest Territory. Finally, however, they were defeated by the United States Army in 1832 and forced into submission. About 1837 the Seminoles in Florida led by Osceola also fought a long and brave but eventually unsuccessful fight against being driven from their homes.

Under the Removal Act, President Andrew Jackson, who was no friend of the red men—he thought it was "ridiculous to deal with the separate tribes as though they were sovereign nations"—was given the right to trade land west of the Mississippi River for land belonging to the Five Civilized Tribes in the southeastern United States. Among these tribes the Cherokees put up the fiercest struggle against removal, but in the end they, too, were forced westward on a tragic winter journey that became known as the Trail of Tears.

By the middle of the nineteenth century—except for a few scattered yet defiant tribes—there was no longer any serious Indian problem in the East and Southeast. The problem, however, had not been solved. It had simply been shifted elsewhere.

Attempts were also made to force Indian tribes from

When the
Western States
Entered the Union

Canada

Washington 1889
Montana 1889
N. Dakota 1889
Oregon 1859
Idaho 1890
S. Dakota 1889
Wyoming 1890
Nebraska 1867
California 1850
Nevada 1864
Utah 1896
Colorado 1876
Kansas 1861
Arizona 1912
New Mexico 1912
Oklahoma 1907
Texas 1845
Mexico

the American Northwest and Southwest into the Indian Territory between the Mississippi River and the Rocky Mountains, or to confine them to reservations. In 1846 the United States acquired the Oregon Territory from Great Britain. White settlers immediately began to pour into this region, and clashes with the northwest Indians immediately occurred. The Puget Sound area was the site of severe fighting in the 1850s, but the red men were soon defeated and banished to the Indian Territory or put on local reservations. Elsewhere in the Northwest the war between the red men and the white men was to continue into the late 1870s when Chief Joseph was to lead his Nez Percé (nay purr say) Indians in a last heroic stand.

The United States had gained control of the Southwest as a result of the Mexican War. In 1847 there were clashes between the Pueblo Indians and white settlers in what is today's New Mexico. The Navajos and Apaches (uh patch eez) also went to war when the white men seized their lands in the 1860s. The Pueblos and Navajos were defeated and forced onto reservations, but the Apaches continued to fight valiantly, until late in the 1880s, under their legendary leader, Geronimo.

The basic flaw in the idea of the Indian Territory as a permanent home for the red men was the fact that it remained the Indians' home only so long as the white man chose to regard it as such. In time the so-called Indian Territory came to include most of the land between the Missouri River and Oregon, from the

Canadian border to Mexico. But as the white men moved through this vast region on their way west to California and Oregon, they began to see that it was more fertile than they had been told it was. Why shouldn't they settle and establish farms right there, they asked themselves, rather than continue the westward trek? When gold was discovered in Montana, Wyoming and Colorado as well as in the Black Hills of the Dakotas and in California, treaties that had been made with the Indians were completely forgotten.

As the thousands of pioneer white families moved into the Indian lands, the buffalo—the Indians' primary source of food, clothing and shelter—began to disappear. Not only were the buffalo killed in great numbers, but the white men's cattle began to take over the buffalo's grazing lands. Worse yet, the white settlers began, as the Indians said, "to turn the grass upside down," with their plows.

The Indians of the western plains fought fiercely not only to protect their hunting grounds but also against being placed on reservations. These Indians, unlike their brothers in the East, had horses, and they rode them magnificently. Horses had been brought to North America by the Spanish in the 1500s. At first the Indians were afraid of these strange, new, four-legged beasts, but in time they learned just how valuable horses could be—both for hunting buffalo and in warfare. In a few short years the plains Indians became as expert on horseback as any trained cavalryman. In fact, many U.S. cavalrymen were frank to admit they had never encountered such skilled and daring horsemen as the plains Indians. Nevertheless, as the inevitable conflicts between the white men and the red men continued, both U.S. Army men and white civilians alike came to think that "the only good Indian is a dead Indian."

Just before the American Civil War began in 1861 there were about 225,000 Indians on the western plains. As protection against any red men who threatened the white settlers and to try and keep the Indians on reservations or confined to the Indian Territory, the U.S. government had assigned some 25,000 Army troops to numerous forts throughout the area. Most of these troops were mounted. They were called dragoons at first but later were known as cavalry. The Indians called them Yellowlegs because of the khaki leggings the cavalry always wore.

Outnumbered as they were, the cavalry could rarely challenge the Indians to pitched battles even if this had been the Indian style of fighting—which it was not. The red men preferred the hit-and-run, guerrilla form of warfare at which they excelled. Not only had they become the world's best horsemen, but they had also become experts in the use of firearms fired at a full gallop. The cavalry, for their part, had to confine their efforts to a kind of police action against the Indian marauders, dashing from their forts to attack the raiding red men, and then hastily returning to the protection of their forts once an action had ended.

When the Civil War began, many of the U.S. Cavalry units had to be withdrawn from the prairies and the plains to take part in the fighting in the East.

Execution of the Thirty-Eight Santee Sioux

PHOTO: MINNESOTA HISTORICAL SOCIETY

Many Indians saw this as their golden opportunity to avenge the countless wrongs done to them by the white man. In the summer of 1862 the Santee Sioux, led by Chief Little Crow, killed more than 700 settlers in the Minnesota River valley area before they were halted in a heroic stand at the town of New Ulm, which was destroyed by fire.

Despite the fact that the Civil War was raging, President Abraham Lincoln authorized Colonel Henry Sibley to raise a force of some 1,600 men, who eventually met and defeated Little Crow and his warriors at Wood Lake. Although most of the defeated Sioux retreated into the Dakotas, Sibley pursued and captured 2,000 of them, 306 of whom were found guilty and sentenced to death for their part in the earlier raids. President Lincoln eventually pardoned most of those found guilty, but late in 1862 some thirty-eight of the Sioux warriors were all hanged simultaneously on an enormous scaffold and gallows at Mankato, Minnesota. The mass hanging was witnessed by men, women and children from throughout the territory.

In the summer of 1864 other tribes of the Sioux nation—the Cheyennes and Arapahoes in Colorado, whose hunting grounds had been destroyed by gold-seeking miners—staged a series of raids against white settlements to obtain food. In retaliation against these raids, Colonel John M. Chivington, a former minister, led a regiment of volunteers against Cheyenne Chief Black Kettle and his people at Sand Creek. Despite the fact that most of Black Kettle's braves were away from the Sand Creek camp at the time, Chivington and his men attacked and mercilessly slaughtered women, children and a number of old men. Later the white militia arrived in Denver proudly displaying numerous Indian scalps and were greeted as heroes.

It was the Sand Creek Massacre that set the entire western plains aflame and led directly to the Fetterman Massacre two years later. It also caused a wave of revulsion to sweep through the eastern part of the United States. When all of the facts of the Sand Creek slaughter became known, Chivington and his men were no longer regarded as heroes but as murderers. By this time the Civil War had ended and the American people were sick to death of bloodshed. Peace, they felt, should come to the western plains just as it had come to the North and South in the brother-against-brother war.

Most of the efforts for making peace with the Indians were put forward by the Bureau of Indian Affairs, which had been established as early as 1824 within the War Department but had been bogged down in bureaucratic red tape ever since. While the Bureau's intentions were undoubtedly good, its accomplishments were few. The very fact that it was a peace-keeping bureau within the War Department often made it seem to be in direct conflict with itself.

The Indian Bureau's main efforts centered around supplying food and clothing to such needy tribes as the Arapahoes. At the same time, however, they also supplied the Indians with arms and ammunition, which the Indians used to attack the U.S. Army.

"Something should be done to stop this foolishness," General Philip Sheridan wrote a friend. "I am ordered to fight these Indians and other generals like yourself are ordered to feed them. Although the Arapahoes are still attacking us, their raiding parties are being issued U.S. Army flour, sugar, and coffee."

The enlisted men of the army had a more cynical way of putting it. "What we do," they said, "is feed 'em in the winter and fight 'em in the summer."

Unfortunately, this tragically absurd situation was to continue all during the Indian Wars, which did not end until a quarter of a century after the Civil War.

3

"Today Is a Good Day to Die!"

War Department officials lost little time in finding someone to blame for the Fetterman Massacre outside Fort Kearny in the winter of 1866. The dead Captain Fetterman could scarcely be blamed. After all, many persons regarded him as a martyred hero. What was needed was a live scapegoat. The scapegoat was Colonel Carrington, the commanding officer of Fort Kearny, despite the fact that for months Carrington had been pleading for reinforcements and additional supplies—including the new breech-loading rifles.

Colonel Carrington was relieved of his command and ordered to return East with his wife and children as well as all of the other women and children at the fort. The party suffered great hardships during its trek east, leaving the fort in the midst of continuing blizzards in which a number of persons were frozen to death.

Silently watching the retreating Colonel Carrington from sheltered vantage points along the Bozeman

Trail were Chief Red Cloud and a large number of Sioux and Cheyenne warriors. The Indians made no attempt to attack the wagon train. They were not so much interested in anyone leaving the fort as they were in the fort's being reinforced, for the red men had no intention of giving up their attempts to destroy Fort Kearny and every other fort along the Bozeman Trail.

Despite the Indians' watchful vigil, reinforcements in large numbers did manage to get through to Fort Kearny from Fort Laramie. Supplies in great quantities were also brought in—including the breech-loading Springfields. Both because of the reinforcements and because of the bitter, snowy, subzero weather, Red Cloud and his braves delayed any attacks until the following summer. Then, on successive days at the end of July and the first days of August, 1867, they decided to make separate but coordinated attacks against two forts, Fort Smith and Fort Kearny. The Cheyennes were to attack the former and the Sioux the latter.

The attack on Fort Smith turned into an immediate disaster for the Indians, despite the fact that over a period of months leading up to the battle the red men had succeeded in capturing most of the soldiers' horses. Before making a direct attack on the fort, the Cheyennes decided to eliminate some fifty soldiers who were cutting hay in a nearby field.

Without warning, the more than 600 Cheyenne braves swooped down on the soldiers, whose only defense was a log corral in which the garrison's few remaining horses were kept. Despite the surprise attack, the soldiers managed to retreat inside this corral, where they set up a withering fire. The Indians, certain that they could overrun this small force, rode right up to the corral and attempted to charge it in a frontal assault. But the corral's defenders were all armed with the new breech-loading, repeating rifles, and the concentrated firepower they produced was overwhelming to the attackers. Only a handful of Indians managed to get inside the corral's walls, and these were killed almost immediately.

The rest of the Indians retreated and attempted to smoke out or destroy the men within both the corral and nearby Fort Smith by setting the hayfield afire. At first the effort looked as if it were going to be successful. The hayfield burned fiercely, the flames roaring some fifty feet in the air and approaching to the very edge of the corral. Then, suddenly—some soldiers thought miraculously—there was a shift in the wind, and the onrushing fire stopped and great billows of smoke were blown into the faces of the attacking red men. Within a few moments the Indians gave up their plans to attack the men in the corral as well as the Fort Smith garrison. Under cover of the smoke the Indians retreated, carrying their dead with them. Some twenty Cheyennes died in the engagement. The soldiers suffered several wounded.

The attack on Fort Kearny also eventually proved to be a failure. Here Red Cloud tried to use the same ruse he and his braves had used against Colonel Carrington and Captain Fetterman the previous year.

All during the summer woodcutters had been working in the pine forest some six miles from Fort Kearny to gather logs for the coming winter. They were guarded by a company of cavalry commanded by Captain James Powell. Powell had been at Kearny at the time of the Fetterman Massacre, but unlike the headstrong Fetterman, Powell was a quiet, methodical officer who had worked his way up through the ranks during the Civil War. Each day when he and his cavalrymen escorted the woodcutters to the pine forest he rehearsed his command on how to react against a sudden Indian attack. Near the pine forest he had built what amounted to a small fortress out of wagons with their wheels removed. These wagon beds he had formed in a circle inside of which food and ammunition were stored. In addition to the wagon beds, logs and sacks of grain strengthened the barricade. At strategic points, holes were bored through the shield formed by the wagon boxes through which rifles could be aimed and fired. Captain Powell expected Red Cloud and his Sioux to attack before the summer was out, and Red Cloud lived up to Powell's expectations.

On a blazing hot morning in early August the woodcutters had just begun their work when a force of more than 1,000 Indians attacked through the woods. Half a dozen woodcutters were immediately killed, but a part of Powell's guard managed to escort the other woodcutters back to Fort Kearny. Powell himself, another officer named Lieutenant John Jenness, and thirty soldiers managed to make their way to the protection of the wagon box fortress.

All of the soldiers expected to die. Thirty-two of them against more than 1,000 of Red Cloud's Sioux and Cheyenne warriors—what other outcome could there be? Nevertheless, Captain Powell went methodically about his business, passing out rifles and ammunition, naming the soldiers who were the best marksmen to act as riflemen as well as the other soldiers who were to reload the spent rifles.

There were 500 Sioux in the first wave of warriors to attack the wagon box fortress. Powell ordered his men not to fire until the very last moment. The men obeyed, waiting until the red men were within fifty yards before opening fire. When the first fusillade sounded, attackers went down in rows. The Indians never faltered in their charge, although they expected some letup in the white men's fire as the soldiers

The Wagon Box Fight
PHOTO: NATIONAL PARK SERVICE

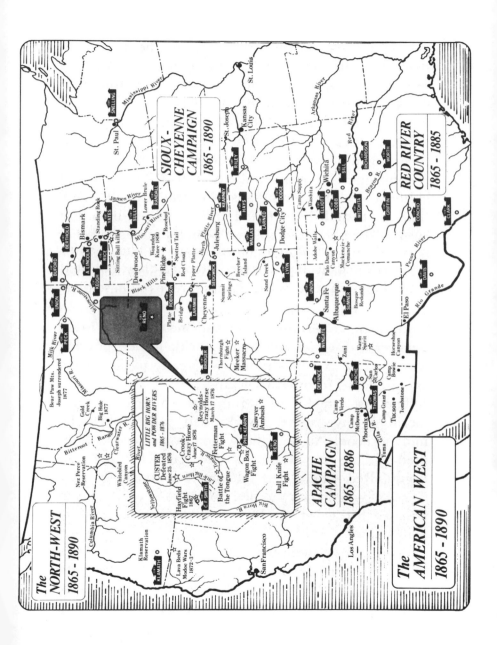

The NORTH-WEST 1865 - 1890

SIOUX-CHEYENNE CAMPAIGN 1865 - 1890

RED RIVER COUNTRY 1865 - 1885

APACHE CAMPAIGN 1865 - 1886

The AMERICAN WEST 1865 - 1890

LITTLE BIG HORN and POWDER RIVERS 1865 - 1876

CUSTER Defeated June 25 1876

Reynolds-Crazy Horse March 17 1876

Hayfield Fight 1867

Crook-Crazy Horse June 17 1876

Fetterman Fight

Sawyer Ambush

Wagon Box Fight

Battle of the Tongue

Dull Knife Fight

33

paused to reload. But there was no hesitancy, no slackening in the rate of fire from the powerful repeating rifles. So powerful were these new rifles that single bullets from them often went through two and three warriors who were hit at close range.

Finally the wave of attackers slowed, halted and then began to retreat. But the retreat was only to re-form their broken ranks and then—as was not customary with the Indians—to attack again. Each time the casualties mounted among the red men, but even so, the handful of soldiers behind the wagon boxes felt there could only be one outcome: They would be overrun by the red men. Most of the soldiers used their revolvers as well as their rifles to fire at the onrushing attackers, but as the day wore on each cavalryman began to make certain that he had one round left in his revolver with which to commit suicide if their position was overrun. No cavalryman was ready to face being captured and tortured to death.

The first attack had begun at seven o'clock in the morning. Five more attacks had taken place by midafternoon. Around the wagon boxes several hundred Indians lay dead. As that day's fighting had begun, Red Cloud had told his assembled warriors, "Today is a good day to die!" All too many had taken him at his word, including Red Cloud's favorite nephew.

Inside the wagon box circle four men had been killed, including Lieutenant Jenness. The twenty-eight who remained lay exhausted under the burning sun, realizing that the next attack would have to be the last.

The men had little or no water to drink, since canteens were steadily emptied onto rifle barrels that had grown red hot from the steady rate of fire. Even if they had the strength to withstand another onslaught, the cavalrymen's ammunition would not hold out. They were down to their last few rounds.

But there was to be no seventh attack. A relief column from Fort Kearny, firing howitzers as it came, finally put the Indians to flight. As the howitzer shells exploded among the retreating red men, the men behind the wagon boxes were too weary to cheer, too weary to rise and greet their rescuers.

Both the Hayfield Fight and the Wagon Box Fight—especially the latter, since it pitted thirty-two soldiers against at least 1,000 red men—went down in U.S. Army military annals as historic battles. Red Cloud and his Sioux and Cheyenne warriors did not regard them as defeats, however, for out of the action on these two days grew a decision on the part of the War Department to close down and evacuate Fort Smith, Fort Kearny and a third bastion, Fort Reno, along the Bozeman Trail. Government officials and civilians in the east were continuing their demands for peace on the prairies, and Red Cloud's price for peace was the closing of the Bozeman Trail. Of the more than 1,000 engagements fought between the U.S. Army and the Indians, between 1865 and 1891, the Hayfield Fight and the Wagon Box Fight were the only ones to result in major, overall victory for the Indians. There were curses and even tears among the cavalrymen who were forced to evacuate the three forts they had so stoutly—and, they thought, successfully—defended. As the cavalrymen rode away, Red Cloud's warriors moved in and burned the forts to the ground.

But once again the peace that came to the prairies was only to be a temporary one. The westward migration of the white man was to continue. In addition to the settlers themselves, telegraph lines had moved relentlessly across the prairies as had horse-drawn express wagons on regular routes and the Pony Express carrying mail; and finally the Iron Horse, or railroad, was about to span the continent. All of these advances were slowly but surely spelling out doom for the red men on the western plains. Once again the red men would resist the westward movement, and once again the U.S. Army would be called upon to fight in the Indian Wars.

4

Manifest Destiny

WANTED: Young, skinny, wiry fellows, not over 18. Must be expert riders willing to risk death daily. Orphans preferred. Wages, $25.00 per week.

Above is a newspaper advertisement that appeared throughout the Midwest early in 1860. It was paid for by the Central California and Pike's Peak Company, which was backed financially by the freight-hauling firm of Russell, Majors and Waddell. Its purpose was to recruit riders for the newly formed Pony Express, a daring venture that was to start at St. Joseph, Missouri, and, using a string of horses and riders in nonstop relays, would carry mail in ten days some 2,000 miles to Sacramento, California. This feat would cut in half the time it took the Southern Overland Express to carry the mail to the west coast by stagecoach.

In addition to the Southern Overland Express, there were numerous similar companies in operation both in

"Faster, Still Faster" was the motto of the Pony Express.
PHOTO: WELLS FARGO BANK HISTORY ROOM, SAN FRANCISCO

the eastern and western United States. These included the Wells Fargo Western Express, the Adams Express, the Butterfield and Wasson Express and the American Express. Only the Southern Overland Express, however, had spanned the continent up to this time.

The Pony Express Company had no problem filling its quota of riders, and the enterprise was an instant if relatively short-lived success. During the eighteen months of its existence the Pony Express employed some 400 fearless young riders who did indeed risk death daily at the hands of the Indians who tried to ambush these early American mailmen all along their route. For protection, riders seldom carried anything more than a knife and a pair of pistols.

The route the Pony Express riders traveled on—short relays of from fifteen to twenty miles at a full gallop—took them from the railhead at St. Joseph to Seneca, Kansas; to Fort Kearny along the Bozeman Trail; to O'Fallon's Bluff, Colorado, along the Oregon Trail; to Julesburg, Colorado; to Salt Lake City, Utah; and then across the Sierra Nevada Mountains and on into Sacramento. From Sacramento the mail was carried by steamer to San Francisco. Traveling the reverse of the St. Joseph-to-Sacramento route, Pony Express riders left Sacramento at the same time riders left St. Joseph, meeting each other at midpoint in crossing the continent.

In the summer of 1861 riders passing through Julesburg, Colorado, didn't realize it, but they were witnessing the completion of a development that would spell the end of the Pony Express. This was the transcontinental telegraph that would be completed in a few short months. The completion of the coast-to-coast telegraph on October 24, 1861, plus the onset of the Civil War ended the Pony Express, but in addition to carrying the mail across the continent in record time, the 400 daring riders were also successful in carrying news to and from the west coast fast enough so that California was able to announce its support of Abraham Lincoln and remain in the Union at the start of the Civil War.

The Pony Express riders carried up to twenty pounds of mail in four pouches attached to a saddle bag, which was called a mochila (moh-chee'-la), a word that was borrowed from Mexico. When a rider and his spent horse reached a relay station, it was the mochila that was thrown across the saddle of the fresh horse that waited eagerly with an equally eager and fresh rider to gallop off on the next relay. Not always, however, was there a new rider at each relay station. Usually, each rider rode from seventy-five to eighty miles but changed horses at each station. The cost of sending a letter via the Pony Express varied between $1 and $5 per half ounce, depending upon the current demand and the time of the year. Only one batch of mail was lost in almost three-quarters of a million miles traveled by the Pony Express. In the end, however, the Pony Express proved to be successful in every way except financially, its backers losing several hundred thousand dollars in the venture.

Another unique venture in the express business at about this time was the Camel Express. Between 1850 and 1860 some 150 Bactrian and dromedary camels were imported by the U.S. Army to haul freight and carry mail in the desert regions of the Southwest. But the camels did not readily adapt to their new way of life or their new masters. Notoriously evil-tempered, the animals proved almost impossible for their American soldier camel drivers to handle, and the experiment was abandoned—to the great relief of both men and beasts.

At the start of the Civil War only the Southern Overland Express continued to travel to and from the west coast carrying mail and freight. It maintained a regular schedule of operations, despite Indian and bandit attacks, right up until the time that the continent was finally spanned by a railroad—an event that was not to occur until the post-Civil War period.

During the Civil War most Americans were forced to forget about the continued expansion of the United States all the way across the Great Plains and on to the west coast and the Pacific Ocean. This continued territorial expansion of the nation had been regarded not only as inevitable by most white Americans but also as something of a sacred racial right. Statesmen of the stature of Thomas Jefferson had often spoken of America's rights of empire that would justify the United States occupying the entire continent.

But it was not until the 1840s and 1850s that people began to say that continued expansion was the nation's "manifest destiny." The popular phrase first appeared in print in a New York City newspaper, the *Democratic Review*, in July, 1845. It was used by the newspaper's editor, John L. O'Sullivan, to proclaim that "It is the fulfillment of our nation's manifest destiny to over-spread the continent allotted by Providence for the free development of our yearly multiplying millions." Soon the words were on everybody's lips, and they were used like a battle cry to justify everything from the annexation of Texas, to the occupation of the Oregon Territory, to making war against Mexico, to the virtual annihilation of the American Indians on the western plains. They were words that would come back to haunt Americans into the twentieth century.

Although manifest destiny was temporarily forgotten during the Civil War, it sprang instantly to life in the form of renewed westward expansion during the postwar period. A Homestead Act, passed during the war in 1862, granted 100 acres of land free to anyone who wanted to settle in the West. Great improvements in farming—including the Oliver plow, the windmill, new harvesting and threshing machines—brought thousands and thousands of pioneers to the Great Plains. Many of these pioneers were ex-soldiers from both the Union and Confederate armies, but hundreds of thousands were immigrants from Europe. Between the end of the Civil War and the start of the twentieth century some 400 million acres of land were occupied by white settlers in the West.

The most spectacular feat in this westward expansion was the building of a transcontinental railway. This effort took four years, with building being done westward from Omaha by the Union Pacific and eastward from Sacramento by the Central Pacific. The construction of the Central Pacific's western portion of the road was perhaps the most difficult. It had to climb more than 7,000 feet over the Sierra Nevada Mountains. In addition, all of its machinery had to be brought to California from the East by way of the Isthmus of Panama or all the way around Cape Horn. The eastern portion of the railroad was almost equally difficult to construct. Here too machinery and material—railroad engines and cars, steel tracks and millions of spikes—had to be brought to the Midwest from the West. Huge supply camps were set up along the right of way, and as soon as the railroad tracks were laid fifty to sixty miles westward, these camps were torn down, loaded onto railroad flatcars and moved westward. And at any moment of the night or day these railroad workers had to be prepared to roll out of their beds or drop their pickaxes and sledgehammers and grab their repeater rifles to fend off an Indian attack. Despite such hardships, morale among the section hands was extremely high, and there was much competition to see which crews could lay track the fastest.

One of the most important problems in this heroic railroad-building effort was supplying the laborers with food. One of the solutions to the problem was the buffalo, upon whom the Indians had depended for centuries. Its meat fed the red men. Its hides clothed and sheltered them. It also occupied a key place in the Indians' religion. Now it began to assume equal importance in the white man's way of life.

To supply the railroad builders with food, U.S.

Buffalo Bill Cody
PHOTO: DENVER PUBLIC LIBRARY, WESTERN HISTORY DEPARTMENT

Army scouts and buffalo hunters were hired to kill buffalo for their meat. Most of the hides were shipped east. Many buffalo had been killed by the white men before this time, but never before in such vast numbers. In the year 1848, for example, a St. Louis company had bought more than 100,000 buffalo robes and some 25,000 tongues, which were considered a delicacy. Within the next few years buffalo hunting became a major industry, and as many as 100,000 hides a day were being sold at auction.

One of the most renowned of all buffalo hunters was a U.S. Army scout, William F. Cody. Born in Iowa on February 26, 1846, Cody had later moved with his family to Kansas. While still in his early teens, Cody had volunteered to become one of those "young, skinny, wiry fellows willing to risk death daily"—a Pony Express rider. During the Civil War he served as a scout with the Union army, but it wasn't until after the war that he came into his own as a buffalo hunter, earning the nickname Buffalo Bill.

Buffalo Bill was so skilled a horseback rider that he could pick up a silver dollar from the ground while riding at a full gallop. And he was so skilled with a rifle that he personally killed more than 4,000 buffalo in a year and a half. There were many other buffalo hunters who were almost Buffalo Bill's equal. In the year 1865 their combined efforts resulted in the killing of as many as 5,000,000 buffalo. The end result was inevitable—the almost total destruction of the Indians' food supply on the western plains. In 1870 a train on the transcontinental railroad was held up for eight hours by a single herd of buffalo that stretched from horizon to horizon. By 1885 the buffalo was almost extinct. During this same period almost $3 million was paid by several Kansas carbon works firms just for buffalo bones alone. The average price paid was $8 a

An American Bison or Buffalo. At one time buffalo roamed the plains in herds that stretched as far as the eye could see. Today only a few scattered herds remain.

PHOTO: DEPARTMENT OF THE INTERIOR

ton, and it took about 100 buffalo carcasses to make one ton of bones. Just in the state of Kansas some 31 million buffalo were slaughtered in a decade and a half.

Even as the buffalo began to disappear from the plains, despite fierce resistance to their slaughter by the Indians, the white men refused to believe that the buffalo was fast becoming extinct. Cody, who later earned a Congressional Medal of Honor for his efforts and became a popular folk hero with his staged Wild West shows, insisted that the great herds had drifted north to Canada or south into Mexico and would soon be back.

Thus, at the cost of the virtual extinction of the buffalo, the great transcontinental railroad was completed. And at the cost of constant conflicts with the Indians who were driven to greater and greater acts of desperation as they saw their lands being taken over by the white man and their hunting grounds being destroyed, America made its way westward along the path of manifest destiny.

The two links of the transcontinental railroad were joined at a place called Promontory Point near Ogden, Utah, on May 10, 1869. Here the presidents of the Central Pacific and Union Pacific railroads, Leland Stanford and Thomas Durant, drove in golden spikes joining the two links. The transcontinental telegraph also played its role in manifest destiny on this day, announcing to the nation and the world that this epic engineering feat had been accomplished. There was a national celebration. Bells and chimes sounded in San

Francisco and New York City. Cannons roared throughout the land. Everywhere there was rejoicing—everywhere, that is, except in the tepees of the lonely and forgotten red men. Soon, however, the white man's rejoicing would be brought to an abrupt halt, as the besieged but undefeated red men returned to the warpath.

5

"Forty Miles a Day on Beans and Hay"

"There are two classes of people who are always eager to start an Indian war—the army and our frontiersmen." So stated an editorial in a New York daily newspaper during the late 1860s.

Actually, no statement could have been further from the truth, especially as far as the army was concerned. Even during periods of peace with the Indians, the life of an army officer or enlisted man on the western plains meant a life of self-sacrifice and virtual exile. When fighting broke out, conditions grew even worse. And yet there was no lack of volunteers for this spartan service, despite the hardships involved.

By 1869 there were some ninety-three U.S. Army forts scattered throughout the West and Southwest. All of them were undermanned, and their garrisons were always fearful of Indian attacks. Rather than planning any long-term, full-scale campaigns against the Indians, all the fort commanders could hope to accomplish was to provide protection for the frontiersmen and women, railroad builders, railroad crews and passengers as they followed the American quest of empire westward.

Although the maximum strength of the army permitted by law during this period was 25,000 men, not all of them were available in the West. Many soldiers were on duty in the south during the post-Civil War Reconstruction period, and others manned coastal fortresses as garrison troops. The presence of manned forts in Indian Territory—the Indians called the forts "war houses"—did to some degree help in keeping the peace in the West. But it was a nervous peace at best, and one that was constantly being broken by sudden

Fort Buford quarters in summer at the turn of the century
PHOTO: DENVER PUBLIC LIBRARY, WESTERN HISTORY DEPARTMENT

murderous flareups. When these flareups occurred, men died. The result was a constant nervous tension that served to make army duty in the West even more nerve-wracking than service in times of traditional warfare. Not all men could stand up under this strain. It took a rare kind of quiet courage for men in the frontier forts to go about their necessary but dull daily routines while maintaining a hair-trigger readiness to go into instant action that might mean death, severe injury or capture and death by torture.

Contrary to popular belief, the frontier army posts of the time were not all walled fortresses. Many of them, from a distance, resembled small villages set down

Fort Abraham Lincoln in winter at the turn of the century
PHOTO: DENVER PUBLIC LIBRARY, WESTERN HISTORY DEPARTMENT

upon the plains. Barracks and other buildings were made out of logs, earth and adobe bricks. Many had dirt floors. Well-established posts had some frame buildings, but construction of these required much additional labor on the part of the soldiers, and even then frame building materials were not readily available.

The officers who commanded these posts were usually ex-Union officers who were veterans of the Civil War. All had taken severe cuts in rank. Ex-Union generals served in grades from colonel on down to lieutenant. Ex-Confederate officers, often under assumed names, served in the ranks as enlisted men.

A few officers had their wives and families with them at these forts. Families, however—and especially those with young children—presented serious problems, and not only because of the Indian menace. When children reached school age, attempts were sometimes made to establish post schools for them, with the better educated wives and mothers acting as teachers. This was seldom satisfactory. Consequently, if children were to obtain an education, they had to be sent back east to school. This meant breaking up the family, sometimes for years on end. It was also expensive, and top-ranking officers' pay was low, ranging from $300 a month for a colonel down to $125 a month for a lieutenant. Promotions were quite rare, a lieutenant often serving for years in grade before being promoted to captain. Attaining the grade of major in twenty-five years was considered a rare achievement.

There was a powerful military caste system in the

army. This was a carry-over from European armies after which the U.S. military system had been fashioned. Officers rarely spoke to enlisted men except in line of duty, and officers and enlisted men almost never mixed socially. In all matters—from pay to quarters to food to disciplinary treatment—there was an enormous gulf between officers and enlisted men, a situation that most recruits deeply resented but could do little about.

Enlisted men's pay ranged from $13 a month for privates up to between $22 and $34 a month for sergeants. They could earn perhaps a dollar a day extra doing menial duties and chores around the post, which gave rise to a line of song the enlisted men chanted: "A dollar a day is damn poor pay, but thirteen a month is less." A few enlisted men also kept their wives with them on the post. These women often worked as laundresses for officers and their wives to earn a few extra pennies. The children of enlisted men were never allowed to attend the same classes as officers' children if there was a school at the army post.

Nevertheless, the backbone of the U.S. Army that fought in the Indian Wars was made up of enlisted men. All were volunteers. Many of them, like their officers, were ex-Civil War soldiers, but a surprisingly large number were civilian immigrants—Irish, Swiss, German, Canadian, French and British. The Irish far outnumbered all other immigrant army enlistees, so far in fact that the New York comedy vaudeville team of Harrigan and Hart sang a song on the subject called "The Regular Army O!" It became a popular hit of the day. One of its verses went:

There was Sergeant John McCaffery
   and Captain Donahue,
Oh, they made us march and toe the mark
   in gallant Company "Q";
Oh, the drums would roll, upon my soul,
   this is the style we'd go:
Forty miles a day on beans and hay
   in the Regular Army O!

The beans, of course, referred to the soldiers' diet and the hay to the cavalry horses' diet, on which both were supposed to be able to travel forty miles a day. Company Q was the designation commonly given to the men who were serving time in the guardhouse for some infraction of regulations.

Few of the enlisted men were educated, and many could not read or write beyond signing their name on a payroll or clothing issue list. Almost all came from poor economic backgrounds. Many of them enlisted because jobs were scarce, and they hoped to be able to learn English well enough to get work after their five-year term of enlistment was up.

All too often raw recruits found themselves on active duty at a frontier post within two or three months after they had enlisted. At the recruit depots in Columbus, Ohio; Jefferson Barracks, Missouri; and David's Island, New York, they had been issued leftover, dark blue Civil War uniforms and obsolete weapons. They had also been introduced to army regulations and been taught close-order marching drill and the manual of arms. Cavalry recruits had also been instructed in

Many army recruits during this period were European immigrants. Typical recruits from Switzerland were Sergeant Conrad Grass (seated) and Private Peter Brosi.

PHOTO: DON LAWSON

mounting and dismounting horses and the care of their animals. Saber drill and most advanced training in the use of weapons had to be learned by harsh experience at the frontier forts.

Although the recruit depots were short on training, they were long on discipline. Orders had to be obeyed instantly and without question. Infractions of even minor regulations were punished by fines and guard-house sentences. Punishment might also include being forced to run around a so-called bull ring, where horses were normally trained, at double and triple time while a sergeant cracked a bullwhip at the heels of men who slowed down. As a result, recruits were not reluctant to leave the training depots for the unknown trials in the West.

They were shipped to their regular duty posts by railroad, wagon and stagecoach. Even if they were cavalrymen, the final stage of their journey might very well include a long, forced march. Along the way their diet consisted of hardtack, bacon and coffee. When they arrived, they were immediately assigned to their new companies, and these companies quickly became the soldiers' "home and family." Soldiers rarely trans-ferred out of their original companies. There was close and jealous comradeship among all the men of a company. Rarely did they make friends with the members of other companies. Each company was a self-sufficient unit, on or off the post, in peace or war. The men trusted one another implicitly. They worked together, ate together, slept together, fought together and all too often died together. The men of each

Headquarters Department of the Platte

OFFICE OF THE INSPECTOR OF RIFLE PRACTICE,

Omaha, Neb., July 8th, 1884

Sergeant C. Grass, of Co. B, 9th Regiment of Infantry, having qualified as MARKSMAN in conformity with requirements prescribed by General Orders No. 12, series of 1884, from Headquarters of the Army, is entitled to wear the Marksman's Buttons until the 30th day of September, 1885.

Inspector of Rifle Practice, Department of the Platte

APPROVED: John Gibbon
Colonel 7th Infantry, Commanding.

QUALIFYING SCORES:

200 yds.	Per cent.	300 yds.	Per cent.	600 yds.	Per cent.
4.4.5.44	84	5.44.5.4	88	2.2.5.4.8	92
4.4.5.54	88	4.5.5.34	84	3.3.4.4.5	76
4.5.3.44	80	4.4.4.44	80	5.0.5.5.5	80

MARKSMAN'S QUALIFICATIONS.—80 per cent. at 200 yards (standing) and 300 yards (kneeling); 70 per cent. at 600 yards (lying). Three scores of five shots each.

Marksman's Certificate
PHOTO: DON LAWSON

company shared a rare common bond that was only broken when their enlistments ended, or by death or desertion.

At their new home the recruits again engaged in close-order drill and performed endless chores called fatigue duty around the post. Everything else they learned about professional soldiering they learned by trial and error, by watching and copying the old soldiers already at the post. In their spare time they polished and cleaned their equipment and weapons under the hard eyes of a corporal or sergeant.

Infantry and cavalry companies numbered about seventy-five men. There were ten companies in an infantry regiment and twelve companies or troops in a cavalry regiment.

Black soldiers who volunteered to remain in the army after the Civil War were organized into the Ninth and Tenth Cavalry regiments, and the Twenty-fourth and Twenty-fifth Infantry regiments. They were commanded by white officers and segregation was rigidly practiced. Occasionally whites and blacks competed in athletic contests, but this was about the extent of their mixing together.

Black soldiers were often called Brunettes, but the Indians called them Buffalo Soldiers, a name the black soldiers accepted proudly. The buffalo was made the central figure in the black soldiers' regimental crests, and throughout the Indian Wars the buffalo crest was widely known as the unique symbol of the brave "blacks in blue."

The common explanation for the term Buffalo

Soldier was that the Indians thought the hair of the black soldiers resembled that of the buffalo. The buffalo was a sacred animal to the red men, and naming their black opponents Buffalo Soldiers was clearly intended as a term of great respect. Buffalo soldier casualties were rarely scalped by the Indians.

The barracks in which the enlisted men—black or white—lived were small and foul-smelling. There was little or no privacy, all of the men bunking together in

Emblem of the Buffalo Soldiers
PHOTO: THE NATIONAL ARCHIVES

one dormitorylike room. Wooden cots with crude mattresses and blankets of wool or buffalo skins were lined up within two or three feet of each other. At the foot of each cot was a footlocker in which the men kept their personal belongings and issue clothing. The privacy of these footlockers was fiercely guarded and rigidly respected. Barracks were heated by wood-burning cast-iron stoves. At night, light was supplied by kerosene lamps and candles.

Food was very important to these frontier soldiers—and a frequent cause of complaint. It varied little and included hash, slumgullion stew, beans, bacon, beef, pork, coffee, sugar, salt, vinegar and molasses. Often the meat was old and rancid and not infrequently crawling with worms. Occasionally there would be stewed dried apples or prunes. The army did not supply milk, butter or eggs, but the soldiers frequently pooled their meager money to buy such "treats." The lack of fresh vegetables was the greatest problem as far as diet was concerned, the army supplying only dried vegetables in large, compressed cakes that could be soaked in water and were regarded by all soldiers as being virtually inedible. As a result, many soldiers had their own post gardens in which they grew fresh vegetables that brought premium prices. Nonetheless, scurvy—caused by a lack of fresh vegetables—occurred frequently, especially during the winter months, at army posts on the frontier. Buffalo meat and fresh game—when it was available, which was seldom—also helped supplement the soldiers' monotonous diet. Canned foods such as sardines, oysters, beef and a few delicacies were sold by post traders, but these were so expensive that few soldiers could afford them.

Unless there was actual warfare with the Indians, the daily routine at a fort on the western plains began each day with reveille and roll call at 6:00 A.M. (There were at least two more roll calls during the day.) Breakfast was at 6:30, and a fatigue period for policing and cleaning up the company area was at 7:30. Fatigue duty might also include stable police, kitchen police or cleaning barracks and acting as room orderlies. Sick call and the assembly of a guard detail took place at 8:30. The assembly of the guard—called guard mount—was always a dramatic time with a band playing and buglers sounding the calls that meant a new guard was relieving the old one that had been on duty for the previous twenty-four hours. The new guard mount was always carefully inspected by a first sergeant, by a sergeant major and finally by the officer of the day.

After guard mount the boots and saddles call was sounded at 10:00, and there followed both mounted and unmounted drill until noon. After the noon mess period there was afternoon drill that usually included target practice and other training in the use of weapons. This lasted until 4:30 when stable call was sounded and the men took care of grooming their horses until it was time for supper or evening mess. (Grain for the horses had to be shipped in from the east at a cost of about $35 a month per horse. Many soldiers insisted that their horses ate better than they did, a complaint that was seldom disputed.)

After supper there was a sunset retreat formation at which the entire garrison was required to appear in dress uniforms. Tattoo was sounded at 9:00 P.M., at which the soldiers were required to assemble in company formation in front of their barracks. Lights out sounded at 9:30, followed by taps a short time later.

Sunday was the only day of the week when soldiers had any free time, and then there was a church call plus a regular weekly inspection that occupied most of the morning. The men could move about the post freely in their free time, but they were expected to be

Mounted infantry on the western plains
PHOTO: DENVER PUBLIC LIBRARY, WESTERN HISTORY DEPARTMENT

always within bugle call, not merely for training formations and roll calls but mainly in case of sudden Indian attack.

Life at these frontier army posts was indeed grim, monotonous and filled with boredom. It was little wonder, therefore, that discipline and desertion became serious problems. Actually, the War Department reported that of all the men recruited between the end of the Civil War and the end of the Indian Wars, one-third had deserted.

The abuse of alcohol was the common cause for soldiers' deserting the army. The dreary daily life and the isolation of army posts led the men to seek relief in liquor, which could be obtained from post traders. Sometimes it was bought or stolen from civilian sources. Paydays usually were times of raucous and drunken celebration. If army posts were located near frontier towns, local saloon keepers saw to it that all the liquor the soldiers wanted was available—until their money ran out. Such celebrations frequently wound up in brawls, and occasionally officers were insulted or physically assaulted. Then, to escape the punishment that was certain to follow, the guilty soldiers often changed into civilian clothes and never returned to duty.

During the 1870s and 1880s, one official army report stated that as many as forty-one out of every 1,000 men, or one out of twenty-five men, were treated for alcoholism. The rate of alcoholism among the black soldiers was far lower—only approximately five cases per 1,000 men.

In most cases the only real cure for such problems was increased physical activity on the part of every man in each garrison as well as strong leadership by officers and noncommissioned officers. Unfortunately, physical activity and brave example reached their greatest peak during defensive stands or campaigns against the Indians. Ironically, as the famous General George Armstrong Custer pointed out, disciplinary problems, the excess use of alcohol and even desertion from duty were at their lowest ebb at the height of the most dangerous periods of warfare with the red men.

6
The Boy General

George Armstrong Custer, the most colorful as well as the most controversial U.S. Army officer of the Indian Wars, had risen rapidly to fame in the Civil War. Long before he and some 225 cavalrymen under his command were killed by the Indians in the Battle of the Little Bighorn in 1876, Custer had been alternately praised as a hero and damned as a villain. The circumstances of his death would only increase the controversy.

Custer was born on December 5, 1839, at New Rumley, Ohio, the son of Pennsylvania Dutch parents. His father was a blacksmith and farmer. Young George was the third of seven children. A younger brother, Thomas, was also to become a soldier, entering the army during the Civil War as a private, attaining a commission, and winning two medals for capturing Confederate battle flags. The two brothers were also to serve—and to die—together during the Indian Wars.

Some historians have said young George wanted to become a soldier from his early boyhood, but there is little evidence to support this. After his mother died, the family moved to Michigan where George was successful in obtaining an appointment to the United States Military Academy at West Point. Certainly his record there failed to indicate that he had any interest in being either a student or a soldier. In 1861 he was graduated from the academy last in his class of thirty-four and with dozens of demerits for undisciplined behavior. Nevertheless, he was immediately pressed into service as a lieutenant in the Second Cavalry Division and saw action in the first Battle of Bull Run at the start of the Civil War.

While his fellow soldiers might criticize Custer as a "show-off and glory seeker," they could not fault him for lack of courage. He was, in fact, fearless to the point of recklessness. His bold daring plus a genuine flair for cavalry combat tactics resulted in his being given the temporary wartime rank (called a brevet) of brigadier general. At twenty-three he was the youngest general in the Union army.

The Boy General, as he was frequently called—and often sarcastically—went on to serve with reckless daring at Gettysburg and in the campaigns in Virginia. As a result, he was promoted to major general and given command of General Philip Sheridan's Third Cavalry Division. He continued to serve gallantly until the end of the war. During the final weeks of the war it was the relentless pressure of Custer's cavalry on General Robert E. Lee that led to the final

Lieutenant Colonel George Armstrong Custer
PHOTO: DENVER PUBLIC LIBRARY, WESTERN HISTORY DEPARTMENT

Confederate surrender at Appomattox. It was Custer who received Lee's white flag of truce offered by the Army of Northern Virginia.

After the Civil War, Custer's rank reverted to that of captain, and his salary was cut by three-quarters. His demotion in rank and pay as well as the lack of excitement in the peacetime army led him to consider becoming a soldier of fortune in Mexico or South America. Although Custer was in constant trouble with his superior officers as well as with the men who served under him, General Sheridan finally succeeded in getting Custer promoted to lieutenant colonel and placed in charge of the newly formed Seventh U.S. Cavalry in 1866. Custer's first major introduction to the Indian Wars was in leading the Seventh Cavalry in an expedition against the Cheyenne Indians.

The expedition against the Cheyennes was decided upon by General Sheridan who had made up his mind—like both Presidents Andrew Jackson and Ulysses S. Grant—that peace with the Indians could not be accomplished by making treaties with them. They must be defeated in battle. He had also decided to do away with the old "fight 'em in the summer and feed 'em in the winter" policy. The red men, Sheridan was convinced, could be defeated in the winter when conditions were at their worst. What was needed was a mobile, fast-moving combat force that could strike against the enemy no matter what the weather. The most mobile of all U.S. Army combat forces was, of course, the cavalry. Now, Sheridan called upon Colonel Custer and his Seventh Cavalry to go into action against the red men as soon as they went into winter quarters.

Custer and his command left Fort Supply in Oklahoma Indian Territory in snowy, subzero weather on November 23, 1868. Always the showman, Custer had the garrison band play a rousing song, "The Girl I Left Behind Me," as he and his troopers streamed out of the fort. Custer also insisted that the band accompany him on this first winter campaign of the Indian Wars.

The Seventh Cavalry had been whipped into a crack cavalry outfit by Custer. Not only were its supply wagons drawn by prize mule teams, but each cavalry company or troop was also mounted on Thoroughbred horses. Several troops rode prize bays; others rode sorrels, chestnuts, grays and blacks. Each troop had horses of a distinctive color. Custer himself rode a Kentucky Thoroughbred given to him by General Sheridan when Custer had assumed command of the Seventh Cavalry.

A horse that was one day to earn undying fame and become a cavalry legend after the Battle of the Little Bighorn was ridden by Captain Myles W. Keogh. This was a spirited bay called Comanche.

Also accompanying the Seventh Cavalry was a detachment of forty sharpshooters, who had been drilled at target practice for the past several weeks by Custer himself.

Although the weather remained snowy and cold, Custer and his command advanced against the Cheyennes without too much discomfort. The supply wagons were able to provide hot evening meals, and all of the troopers were well equipped with blankets and buffalo robes so they could keep warm at night. Custer's only complaint was the lack of wild game along their route. He had brought with him a pack of English hunting dogs and was disappointed over not being able to use them. Finally he and his staghounds did manage to bring down a small buffalo, which was served to the officers' mess.

Custer had been told by scouts that the Cheyennes were camped somewhere in the valley of the Washita River. He had not been told, however, who was the chief in command of the red men's winter encampment. This chief was Black Kettle, many of whose people had been massacred at Sand Creek. After the Sand Creek Massacre it had been rumored that Black Kettle had died along with many Cheyenne old men, women and children, but this rumor had later been proved false. At the time of the attack, he had been away from the Sand Creek camp along with his many braves.

Following the Sand Creek affair, Black Kettle had staged numerous raids of revenge against the white man, but within recent months he had given every indication that he was willing to accept a peace treaty and perhaps live on a reservation. But General Sheridan had now given up on peace treaties, and Custer was to impress upon the red men that all resistance against the whites was futile.

Custer and his command advanced for several days toward the Washita River. Occasionally they lost their way, but Custer took over from the scouts and made his own new compass readings, correcting the direction in which they were traveling. Scouts with Custer were impressed with his leadership and military abilities.

When he was convinced the enemy was not too far off, Custer sent Major Joel Elliott forward with a scouting party. Elliott soon sent back a messenger to report that he had located the enemy. Custer ordered his command forward at the double, and within a few hours they were looking down from a high ridge at Black Kettle's camp in the river valley below. Custer quietly disposed his troops and told them they would attack at dawn.

Actually the red men's winter encampment was much larger than the part of it that Custer and his men could see. Beyond a bend in the river were other camps of Kiowas, Arapahoes and plains Apaches.

At dawn the next day the peaceful quiet of the winter's morning was rudely shattered by several buglers sounding "Charge!" and almost before Black Kettle and his people could roll out of their blankets Custer's Seventh Cavalry had burst upon them. Men, women and children were shot down indiscriminately. Black Kettle himself had managed to get to the doorway of his tent, where he stood prepared to defend his family. The old chief went down in the first fierce fusillade, as did his wife standing immediately behind him. Somewhat later, Black Kettle's teenaged son was cut down with a saber stroke by an officer whose name would later be recorded for history among those slain at the Battle of the Little Bighorn—Captain Frederick Benteen.

Captain Frederick Benteen
PHOTO: DENVER PUBLIC LIBRARY, WESTERN HISTORY DEPARTMENT

The indiscriminate slaughter—Custer lost only a handful of wounded—had gone on for less than an hour when the braves from the encampments farther down the Washita Valley launched a counterattack through the bloodstained snow. But Custer quickly deployed his men in a defensive battle formation and ordered the sharpshooters into action. The hail of their accurate fire beat back the Indian attack. It was probably during this part of the battle that Major Elliott and a detachment of men got cut off from the main force.

Once the attacking braves had been beaten back, Custer ordered his men to systematically set about destroying everything in sight—tents, lodges, more than a thousand buffalo robes, a thousand pounds of lead and gunpowder and several thousand arrows. So there could be no pursuit, Custer even ordered the killing of some 700 Indian ponies. Reluctantly, the cavalrymen, who prized horses, carried out this last order.

Now, however, Custer was fully aware of the number of additional Indians there were beyond Black Kettle's camp, and he was faced with the problem of getting his command out of what had become a virtual trap. Once again Custer's daring proved equal to the occasion. Forming his troopers and supply wagons into a long column, he ordered the regimental band to strike up "Ain't I Glad to Get Out of the Wilderness," and marched his column right into the face of the remaining Indians. The red men could not believe that Custer would dare to march his men directly toward them unless the cavalry greatly outnumbered the red men, so they retreated. After they had retreated, Custer reversed his order of march back toward Fort Supply.

As Custer made his way to Fort Supply, several of his aides suggested that they should search for Major Elliott and his lost detachment, but Custer refused to risk the rest of his command to do so. Later Custer was severely criticized for this decision—especially when the mutilated bodies of Elliott and his men were found several weeks later not far from Black Kettle's village.

Thus ended Custer's first stand in the Indian Wars.

Custer's first stand proved Sheridan's contention that the cavalry could successfully "fight 'em" in both winter and summer. And Sheridan lost little time in following up on this initial success. Just as Custer had systematically destroyed the supplies in Black Kettle's village, so Sheridan set about pursuing other Indian tribes in an effort to destroy them or force them onto reservations.

For the most part Sheridan was successful. There were, however, certain major geographic areas where the Indians fought on valiantly if futilely well into the 1880s. They included the West and Northwest, where the Apaches under Geronimo and the Nez Percés under Chief Joseph were to make their last, embittered stands. But before they could be subdued, the U.S. Army had to wipe out all remaining resistance in the Indian Territory and on the Great Plains.

In the early 1870s a major area of resistance extended from Texas well into the Indian Territory.

Here the Comanches and the Kiowas—the latter under the great chief Satanta—were proud of having killed more white men than several other tribes combined, and they made it clear that they were out to run up an even greater score.

General William Tecumseh Sherman, like Sheridan a great Union army Civil War hero, was given the task of bringing Satanta to terms. (Ironically, Sherman, the Indian fighter, had been given his middle name after an Indian, the Shawnee chief, Tecumseh.) Sherman succeeded in doing this by using a ruse to trick Satanta into attending a peace parley at Fort Sill in 1871. There Satanta was rudely handcuffed and carried off to Texas as a prisoner. But the Indian Bureau, much to Sherman's and Sheridan's disgust, succeeded in talking the Texas governor into releasing the Kiowa chief.

Sherman told the governor he hoped Satanta would one day lift the governor's scalp by way of thanks. This did not happen, but Satanta did return to the warpath during the bitter Red River War that soon erupted.

7
The Red River War

"If any man is killed, I'll make him a corporal!"

Those were the wry words shouted by Captain Adna R. Chaffee to his squadron of cavalry as they charged into battle against several hundred Cheyennes, Comanches and Kiowas on August 30, 1874. This was the opening engagement in the Red River, or Staked Plains, War.

For several months during the winter of 1873–74 the three tribes had gone on the warpath in Texas. Their bloody raids were climaxed in the spring and summer of 1874 with attacks at a number of places in the Texas Panhandle. Finally, General Sherman was given orders to end Indian troubles in this area once and for all. Sherman in turn gave orders to General Sheridan to go into action.

Sheridan's plan was to launch a multipronged cavalry and infantry campaign against the Indians, converging on them from half a dozen different directions. These converging cavalry and infantry columns numbered several thousand men, but their combined strength was never brought into action at one time. Indian warrior forces in the Panhandle were about 1,200 strong, but they, too, were broken up into smaller bands of braves.

Both sides suffered severely from drought conditions and from a locust plague that struck the southern plains during the summer. As one column of cavalry and infantry marched south toward the Panhandle, the heat became so intense and water was so scarce that the troopers wet their lips with blood from gashes they cut in their own arms.

This column, under the overall command of Colonel Nelson Miles, numbered 750 men. They encountered their first hostiles, 200 Cheyenne braves, in hilly country north of a fork in the Red River near the Staked Plains. Colonel Miles immediately ordered his infantry and cavalry to attack. It was at this point that Captain Chaffee made his offer of a corporal's stripes to any man killed in action. The Indians made several prospective promotions available in the first moments of the battle.

Despite the fact that they were badly outnumbered, the Indians fought valiantly, giving up ground only a few desperate yards at a time. Miles's intention was to drive the red men out onto the relatively barren flats of the Staked Plains where there would be little conceal-ment. There he hoped to surround them and force them to surrender.

As the battle continued, the Indians received rein-forcements from Comanches and Kiowas in the nearby

General Nelson A. Miles
PHOTO: DENVER PUBLIC LIBRARY, WESTERN HISTORY DEPARTMENT

hills until their total number almost equaled the army force. But Miles had at his command a number of small cannons which he had placed strategically in the hills. They could be fired directly down onto the Indians with devastating effect. Slowly, relentlessly, the infantry and cavalry forced the Indians out onto the Staked Plains.

Although Miles had now accomplished his first goal, he was unable to follow up on his initial success because his own men were totally exhausted from the heat and lack of water. He was also short of supplies. Consequently, Miles decided to break off the engagement and camp near a branch of the Red River known as Prairie Dog Fork.

Early in September the drought finally broke, and the entire area turned into a sea of mud in which both the white men and the red men could scarcely move. Temporarily, pursuit was out of the question.

Meanwhile, another cavalry column from the west under Major William Price and a third column from the south under Colonel Ranald Mackenzie had also moved into the Staked Plains region. What Miles now feared was that one of these columns would encounter the main body of hostiles before Miles and his force could get back into action. It was generally believed that Chief Satanta was leading a large Kiowa war party, and Miles wanted the honor of capturing him. But before anyone had a chance to capture Satanta, the chief quietly surrendered. Why he did so was not too clear, but it appeared that he wanted to save the women and children in his tribe from further harassment.

Following Satanta's surrender, both Price and Mackenzie continued their search for the main body of red men. The torrents of rain continued—because of the weather, the Indians called it "The Wrinkled Hands campaign"—but Mackenzie managed to keep his column moving through the mud by sheer will-power and determination. He drove his men ruthlessly. When his supply wagons became mired down, he ordered his infantry and cavalry to carry the supplies on their backs, abandoning the wagons in the mud.

Late in September, Mackenzie's column encountered large numbers of hostiles, as the Indians were usually called, many of whom attempted to steal the cavalry horses. Mackenzie's men beat off the attackers, however, and prepared to mount an attack of their own. On September 28 Mackenzie cornered several hundred families of Kiowas, Comanches and Cheyennes in a place called Palo Duro Canyon at the edge of the Staked Plains. Mackenzie ordered his men to climb down the sides of the canyon hand-leading their horses, but before the cavalry could assemble on the canyon floor and mount an attack, the Indians began to flee, leaving their horses behind them. Instead of pursuing the Indians, Mackenzie ordered that all tepees, other shelters, food and equipment be destroyed. Mackenzie's men then herded some 1,500 Indian ponies out of the canyon. Once outside, Mackenzie let his men pick out several hundred of the best ponies. The rest—at least 1,000 horses—he ordered destroyed. The red men now had no choice but surrender.

With equal ruthlessness Sherman and Sheridan continued to apply pressure on the Indians throughout the Red River and Staked Plains area. Gradually the pressure became so overwhelming that one after another the tribes either surrendered or drifted back onto their reservation or they were destroyed. Even life on the reservation seemed preferable to the constant harassment of U.S. Army troops. In 1875 there were mass surrenders, and finally in the spring the bitter campaign ended in total defeat for the Indians. Never again would they go on the warpath in this area.

Satanta was returned to a jail cell in the Texas penitentiary. He remained there until March 1878 when he killed himself by jumping out of a window from the cell block's top floor.

A number of other ringleaders of this uprising were also severely punished. Thirty-three Cheyenne leaders, twenty-seven Kiowas and eleven Comanches were shipped off to prison at St. Augustine, Florida. Many of them died there. Those who survived were freed in

Tomahawk
PHOTO: DENVER PUBLIC LIBRARY, WESTERN HISTORY DEPARTMENT

1878. Most of them returned to their reservation homes, but a handful remained in St. Augustine. They stayed there to work with a U.S. Army lieutenant, Richard Pratt, who had dealt kindly with them while they were in prison and had tried to establish a model system of education for Indians. In 1879 Pratt, again with the aid of his Indian volunteers, established the Carlisle Indian School at Carlisle, Pennsylvania. The school was supported by the U.S. government until 1918, and it was there that Jim Thorpe, one of the most famous athletes in history, began his great career.

With the total defeat of the Kiowas, Cheyennes and Comanches in the Red River War on the southern plains there still remained the great Sioux nation as a major threat on the great plains. The Sioux were led by three of the most powerful chiefs in Indian history —Sitting Bull, Crazy Horse and Gall. It was against these chiefs and their Sioux braves at a site near the Powder River in the valley of the Little Bighorn that Custer was to make his last stand of the Indian Wars.

8
Death of
the Boy General

One of Colonel Custer's favorite officers in the Seventh Cavalry was Captain Myles Keogh, a devil-may-care Irish soldier of fortune who had fought in numerous European battles before coming to the United States during the American Civil War. In the Civil War, Keogh joined the Union army as a captain of volunteers and served as an aide to General George McClellan. After Appomattox, Keogh joined the Regular U.S. Army as a cavalry officer. Dark, curly-haired, and handsome, Captain Keogh's happiest moments were those spent by the side of Colonel Custer, their horses racing stride for stride across the western prairies during a cavalry charge.

Like all good cavalry officers, Keogh had several fine Thoroughbred mounts, but his favorite horse was not a Thoroughbred. It was a somewhat nondescript bay gelding bought for $90 from the government quartermaster corps at St. Louis. Keogh had named the huge charger Comanche, and the horse lived up to his name with continuous displays of courage and blind loyalty to his master. Together, Captain Keogh and Comanche were to ride into cavalry history.

During the summer of 1874, Colonel Custer, Captain Keogh and a small detachment of cavalry were on a scouting expedition in the Black Hills of the Dakota Territory when they discovered outcroppings of gold along a small stream. Custer was somewhat reluctant to report these findings because he knew that a gold rush would result, and this would mean more trouble with the Sioux. Several years earlier, Sioux Chief Red Cloud had reluctantly signed a major peace treaty at

Comanche and Captain Myles Keogh
PHOTO: DENVER PUBLIC LIBRARY, WESTERN HISTORY DEPARTMENT

Fort Laramie in which it was agreed that he and his Sioux warriors would move onto a reservation in the Dakota Territory. In return the U.S. Army was to protect the Sioux reservation from intrusion by the white man. Many of the Sioux had not agreed with Red Cloud's decision and had refused to go onto the reservation. Others who did accept his decision did so with many misgivings. The white man had always broken his promises in the past if it suited his convenience to do so.

It suited the white man's convenience to do so once again when word got out about the discovery of gold in the Black Hills. In 1875 there was a wild stampede in the rush for gold. Mines were dug, towns were built, thousands of get-rich-quick white men streamed into the Territory in total disregard for the red man's rights. Both the Indians and the U.S. Army seemed unable to cope with the problem of maintaining peace on the western plains.

Among the Indian chiefs who had refused to go onto the reservation were a medicine man (called a shaman) named Sitting Bull and two famed battle leaders, Crazy Horse and Gall. Sitting Bull worked his warriors into a frenzy by prophesying that the final clash between the white and red races was now at hand.

When news of the threatened mass Sioux uprising reached the Indian Bureau in Washington, the Indian commissioner, George Stevens, ordered all of the Sioux onto their reservation by the end of the year. Since this order wasn't issued until early in December, 1875, it could not possibly be fulfilled even if the Indians had

Sitting Bull
PHOTO: DENVER PUBLIC LIBRARY, WESTERN HISTORY DEPARTMENT

Gall
PHOTO: DENVER PUBLIC LIBRARY, WESTERN HISTORY DEPARTMENT

wanted to do so—and most did not. When the order was not obeyed, Commissioner Stevens turned the problem over to the U.S. Army.

On March 1, 1876, General George Crook with ten troops of cavalry and two companies of infantry set off across the snow-swept plains from Wyoming's Fort Fetterman to destroy the hostiles.

General Crook was one of the most successful of the Indian fighters, but on this occasion he and his men more than met their master in the person of Crazy Horse. After a two-week forced march, Crook encountered his first hostiles. Dividing his command, Crook sent six troops of cavalry after the small band of Indians, ordering the cavalry under Captain John J. Reynolds to attack and destroy any winter encampments they encountered.

Reynolds and his men advanced during the night, discovering an Indian village at dawn. Attacking quickly, Reynolds achieved only partial surprise and the red men escaped to a nearby forest. Nevertheless, Reynolds struck an all but crippling blow when he burned the village to the ground, destroying all supplies, buffalo robes and shelter, and even capturing most of the Indians' ponies. At midwinter on the barren plains the red men's cause seemed hopeless—and it would have been had it not been for the village's chieftain, Crazy Horse.

Crazy Horse and a number of his best braves had managed to ride out of the doomed village on their ponies. Crazy Horse now rallied the men with horses and prepared a counterattack. Those without horses he told to follow up the initial attack on foot. Then, with total disregard for his own safety, Crazy Horse led the Indian charge right into the heart of the smoking remains of the village and the mounted cavalry.

Reynolds and his men were completely surprised by a counterattack from an enemy they had assumed was totally defeated. But there was nothing defeated about these wildly attacking braves led by a chief whose reckless courage seemed matched only by his luck. Three times Crazy Horse had horses shot out from under him, and three times he remounted a riderless pony from whose back either an Indian or one of the Yellowlegs had been shot. Crazy Horse's personal example of courage seemed to inspire his braves to equal feats of valor. Soon Reynolds, whose forces greatly outnumbered the Indians, found himself all but trapped in a chaotic general engagement. Reynolds was a smart enough officer to realize he could not possibly win this fight, so he ordered his trumpeter to sound the disengagement call. In a matter of moments he and his men were in full retreat to rejoin General Crook.

But Crazy Horse and his braves were not about to stop now. They followed hard on the heels of the white cavalry and soon were able to recapture all of their ponies. By the time Reynolds was able to rejoin Crook, the cavalry was fighting a fierce rearguard action to prevent their entire force from being overrun.

With Reynolds's and Crook's forces once again combined, however, the red men faced too formidable a foe to continue their heroic action. Nevertheless, it

Colonel Thomas Custer
PHOTO: DENVER PUBLIC LIBRARY, WESTERN HISTORY DEPARTMENT

was Crazy Horse and his braves who struck a final blow that resulted in Crook's complete rout. By another daring maneuver Crazy Horse managed to capture the entire herd of cattle upon which the army depended for food. When this deed had been accomplished, Crook had no choice but to return in shame to Fort Fetterman, his winter campaign against the Sioux a complete failure. For his part, Crazy Horse and his braves had not only lived to fight the white man another day but by capturing the herd of cattle had saved all of their people from starvation on the wintery plains.

And this was far from being Crazy Horse's final victory.

The U.S. Army now decided to mount an all-out campaign against the Sioux during the summer of 1876. The campaign was to consist of a two-pronged maneuver with General Crook moving north from Fort Fetterman toward the Rosebud River and General Alfred Terry moving westward from Fort Abraham Lincoln, which was near today's Bismarck. This maneuver, if successful, would catch the Sioux in a pincers somewhere in the area of the Little Bighorn River.

General Crook was the first to make contact with the Sioux, who were—much to Crook's misfortune—once again led by Crazy Horse. On June 17 near the Rosebud River, Crook and fifteen troops of cavalry and five companies of infantry ran head on into an Indian force of approximately equal size and were stunningly defeated. Heroics were performed by both sides in the day-long summer's battle, but in the end it was Crazy Horse's generalship and blazing courage that tipped the balance in the Indians' favor. The next day Crook once again began a retreat to Fort Fetterman.

Although Crazy Horse had now won his second major battle against the white cavalry and infantry, the army's campaign against the Sioux was by no means over. General Terry was also an Indian fighter of renown, and as his second in command he had none other than the celebrated Colonel George Armstrong Custer and Custer's Seventh Cavalry.

Terry's plan seemed simple enough. Reaching the Rosebud River on June 22, he knew the main body of Sioux was somewhere in the valley of the Little Bighorn. But just where they were and how strong they were he did not know. Nevertheless, he ordered Custer and his Seventh to move up the Rosebud River to the Little Bighorn's headwaters. Once at the headwaters, Custer was to move rapidly downstream through the valley until he and Terry's forces met. Terry, of course, was planning to move up the valley of the Little Bighorn. Once again the idea was to catch the Indians in a pincer movement.

All of this seemed clear enough—but for one thing. Custer was told he could use his own judgment and change the plan if something unforeseen occurred. This was to prove a fatal error.

Custer had no intention of letting General Terry reach the Sioux hostiles first. Within recent months several of the nation's leading politicians had been boosting Custer as a candidate for the U.S. presidency in the next election to replace Ulysses S. Grant. The Boy General's name was already widely known, but a ringing victory over the Sioux nation would make Custer's name a household word.

Custer and the Seventh Cavalry jauntily moved up the valley of the Rosebud on June 23, 1876. By the morning of June 25 they found themselves on a high divide between the Rosebud and Little Bighorn rivers. Although Custer didn't yet know where the main body of the Sioux was, Crazy Horse and Gall and their warriors had scouts out to observe every move of the blond Custer. Yellow Hair, as the Indians called Custer, was thoroughly hated by the red men, but they did not underestimate him as a ruthless foe.

All that morning Custer moved forward at a slow but steady pace. Nearby rode Captain Keogh astride Comanche. Custer had now divided his command into three separate units with himself in charge of one battalion, Major Marcus Reno in charge of a second and Captain Frederick Benteen in charge of the third. Near Custer, in addition to Captain Keogh, rode Custer's brother, Tom, and not far away was his brother-in-law, Lieutenant James Calhoun.

Early in the afternoon Custer's and Reno's battalions—they were moving forward within close range of each other—discovered the main Indian camp on the banks of the Little Bighorn.

Custer immediately ordered Reno into the valley to attack the camp.

"If you get into trouble, my whole outfit will support you," Custer told Reno.

Major Marcus Reno
PHOTO: DENVER PUBLIC LIBRARY, WESTERN HISTORY DEPARTMENT

However, as soon as Reno and his men moved into the valley, Custer decided not to enter the valley behind or near Reno but instead to move out around Reno in a somewhat circular fashion, with the apparent intention of attacking the Indians from the rear.

Meanwhile, Captain Benteen had been separated by some distance from both Custer and Reno as he and his men searched through the Bad Lands to the south for the Indians. When he gave up on trying to contact the red men, Benteen ordered his men to link up once again with Reno and Custer. Fortunately, by re-entering the valley of the Little Bighorn, Benteen was able to save Reno's command which had encountered the Indians and was about to be massacred by the hostiles, who outnumbered the whites several to one. Reno's battalion had already suffered severe losses as it was driven across the Little Bighorn River to a ridge on the eastern side. Reno, reinforced by Benteen, managed to withstand fierce attacks by the red men all that night and during most of the following day.

When the remnants of Reno's and Benteen's commands were aware that the siege had suddenly been lifted on the afternoon of June 26, they could not at first figure out the reason. Then they realized that the Indians had streamed away westward as General Terry's larger force came into sight moving up the Little Bighorn. But what was still puzzling to Reno and Benteen was why Custer had neither come to their rescue—as he had told Reno he would do—or why he had not sent word of his own battle situation if he had indeed engaged the Indians. The next day the mystery was solved.

On June 27, 1876, the bodies of Custer and more than 200 of his Seventh Cavalry were found strewn about the battlefield where they had fallen. All of the bodies except that of Custer were mutilated almost beyond recognition.

Little was ever learned of what exactly had befallen Custer and his men. Obviously he and his troopers had stumbled into a much larger Indian force and had been quickly annihilated by Crazy Horse and Gall, who could easily claim the most famous defeat of the white man in the Indian Wars.

As General Terry, Major Reno, Captain Benteen and their men moved sorrowfully about the site of Custer's last stand and began digging shallow graves for the fallen, they were startled to find but one living thing moving on the Custer battlefield. Not far from the fallen body of a captain they could only assume was that of Captain Keogh stood his faithful horse, Comanche. The animal was obviously so much more dead than alive that the Indians had not even bothered to take Comanche with them when they rode off with the rest of the surviving cavalry ponies.

Now Comanche stood, head bowed, his rider's saddle swung awkwardly underneath the horse's belly. He was terribly wounded and seemed about to drop dead himself beside Captain Keogh's body.

Someone suggested shooting the cruelly wounded animal. General Terry curtly refused the suggestion. Instead he ordered that everything possible be done for the stricken horse. His orders were immediately carried out. After his wounds were dressed, Comanche

Crazy Horse
PHOTO: DENVER PUBLIC LIBRARY, WESTERN HISTORY DEPARTMENT

was put aboard a wagon and carried back to Fort Abraham Lincoln. There, for a year, Comanche slowly recovered, a sling supporting him in his stall since he was unable to stand unaided. The commanding officer issued orders for Comanche never to be ridden again or to be put on a work detail. Instead, he was hand-led at the front of all Seventh Cavalry parades and ceremonial marches. With this loving care Comanche not only fully recovered but also lived for fifteen more years, the pet of everyone on the post. When he died in 1891, Comanche's body was stuffed and mounted as a memorial to the U.S. Army Cavalry. He can be seen today at the Natural History Museum on the campus of the University of Kansas.

Crazy Horse's third great victory, the total destruction of Custer's battalion, closed the U.S. Army's campaign against the Sioux in 1876. This did not mean, of course, that the all-out war against the Sioux had ended. In a very real sense it had just begun.

Ironically, the Custer massacre occurred within a few days of the centennial celebration of the birth of the United States as a nation on July 4, 1776. Few white Americans, however, paused to consider that it was now the Indians who were fighting against oppression just as the white colonists had fought for their independence from Great Britain just 100 years earlier. Instead, buildings throughout the land were draped in funeral black in mourning for Custer and his band of intrepid cavalrymen, and people everywhere vowed vengeance against the Sioux.

Late in 1876, General Philip Sheridan assigned the task of forcing the Sioux into submission to Colonel Nelson Miles. Miles set about his task in a methodical, businesslike fashion, determined to harass the Indians without letup until they surrendered or were exterminated. In January, 1877, Miles and his men fought several running battles with the Sioux, inflicting defeats and heavy losses on them at Red Water and Hanging Woman's Fort. By early February the Indians, who were not allowed to go into winter quarters but were kept constantly on the move and on the defensive, began to indicate they were tired of the war.

Late in February a number of Sioux surrendered at the Cheyenne Agency in the Dakota Territory. From that point on into the spring bands of starving Sioux numbering from thirty to several thousand continued to turn themselves in, give up their ponies and permit themselves to be placed under arrest at whatever army post seemed convenient across the western plains. Finally, during the first week in May, Crazy Horse himself with some 1,000 Sioux and 2,000 ponies rode into Fort Fetterman and there surrendered to his old enemy, General Crook. With the surrender of Crazy Horse the Sioux war seemed to be ended.

9
Last Stand
of the Nez Percés

While the last of the great Sioux war parties were being driven from the western plains, other brave bands of Indians were also making their own courageous last stands in the American Northwest and Southwest. These included the Nez Percés, led by Chief Joseph, and the Apaches, led by Geronimo.

The Nez Percé Indians in Idaho, Oregon and Washington were proud of the fact that they had never killed a white man or broken their word—until 1877, just a year after the Custer Massacre. As a matter of fact, when the first white explorers, Meriwether Lewis and William Clark, had ventured into the Columbia River area in 1805 in search of a land route to the Pacific Ocean, they had been greeted in friendly fashion by the Nez Percé Indians. Another early white pathfinder, John C. Frémont, was also warmly received by the Nez Percés when he explored the Columbia River country in 1843.

The name of the Nez Percés—meaning "pierced

noses"—was first recorded by Lewis and Clark in their journals. The name probably was first used, however, by early French-Canadian fur traders who observed an occasional Indian of this tribe who had pierced his nose and decorated it with shells or wampum. It was not the custom of the entire tribe to follow this practice.

Lewis and Clark also noted what magnificent horses the Nez Percés owned and how superbly they rode them. Both the Nez Percés and their closely related kin, the Cayuse tribe, were famed for the horses they succeeded in breeding from those originally acquired from the Spanish. Even today in the western United States the term "cayuse" refers to an Indian pony. Interestingly, even though they were a peace-loving tribe, the Nez Percés were also famed far and wide as sharpshooters with the rifle.

Despite their long record of peaceable dealings with the white man , the discovery of gold in their territory spelled trouble for the Nez Percé Indians just as it had spelled trouble for the Sioux. Shortly after the middle of the century the United States government, at the urging of white settlers in the Northwest, began taking rich and fertile land away from the Nez Percés and forcing them onto a reservation in northwestern Idaho. In 1868, having already given up most of their territory, the Nez Percés signed a treaty with the United States which was to give them territory rights in their ancestral home, the Wallowa Valley in Oregon. Ironically, this was to be the last of some 370 treaties between the United States and the American

Chief Joseph
PHOTO: DENVER PUBLIC LIBRARY, WESTERN HISTORY DEPARTMENT

102

Indians. (The first had been signed with the Delaware Indians in 1778 during the American Revolution.) Up to this time 369 treaties had been broken by the white man. The 370th, the one made with the Nez Percés, was to prove equally worthless.

After the signing of this treaty, President Ulysses S. Grant issued an executive order barring all white settlers from the Wallowa Valley. Then, in the early 1870s, gold was discovered in Nez Percé territory, and treaties and executive orders were promptly forgotten. Once again a movement got under way to force all of the Nez Percés onto the Idaho reservation.

One chief stoutly resisted this move. This was Chief Joseph, a thirty-seven-year-old leader who had never fought a battle with the white man. Nevertheless, in the campaign that followed he was to prove himself a military commander of genius and one who was greatly admired by his white foe.

Joseph continued to resist his people's removal from the Wallowa Valley until 1877. Then he was ordered onto the reservation by the U.S. government, and the U.S. Army's only one-armed general, Oliver O. Howard—he had lost an arm in the Civil War—was directed to see to it that the order was carried out.

Finally, bowing to the inevitable, Chief Joseph agreed to move his people along with their horses and cattle out of the valley. But several of his young braves refused to leave peaceably. They went rampaging up and down the valley, killing some nineteen white settlers and burning their homes. General Howard immediately ordered two companies of cavalry to attack the Nez Percé camp. Despite the fact that they were outnumbered two to one, the sharp shooting Indians had only two braves suffering from slight wounds when the short, bitter battle ended. Howard's cavalry suffered thirty-four troopers killed.

Chief Joseph, however, was tragically aware of the fact that the only hope for him and his people now was to try and escape, perhaps into Canada, before Howard and his command could recover and retaliate. Ordering an immediate forced march, Chief Joseph led his braves and their wives and children on the beginning of what was to be one of the most heroic fighting retreats in military history.

The retreat began in mid-July, 1877. Chief Joseph had at his command no more than 300 fighting braves plus an equal number of women and children. The braves were outnumbered at least four to one in many of the battles fought during the next several months against several separate army commands over a distance of almost 2,000 miles.

A few days after the Indians headed their ponies eastward along the Lolo Trail that began in northwestern Idaho, General Howard ordered his troopers to follow the hostiles in hot pursuit. Almost immediately the Nez Percés were faced with the difficult problem of crossing the Rocky Mountains. They managed to make this crossing before Howard's troops could catch up with them, but when they reached the opposite side of the rocky range and came into the Bitter Root Valley, they ran head on into a small detachment of 100 U.S. troops under Captain C. C. Rawn, who had been sent orders by the newly installed telegraph to intercept the Nez Percés. Rawn had ordered his men to dig entrenchments directly in the face of the oncoming Indians to prevent their continued progress.

Chief Joseph knew he could not risk a frontal assault on the entrenched troops, so he went forward under a flag of truce to parley with Rawn. Rawn's terms for peace were the surrender of all the Indians' arms, ammunition and ponies.

During the parley Chief Joseph realized that although Rawn's forces were skillfully entrenched, they were few in number. Joseph broke off the talks for a conference with his braves and told them the situation. The Indians then decided on a bold, do-or-die move. Feeling certain that Rawn would not risk ordering his troops out of the relative safety of their trenches to engage in a hand-to-hand fight, Joseph and his braves decided simply to walk around the trenches and move on down the valley. This they did, making certain that their detour kept them well out of range of the soldiers' rifles.

The bold maneuver worked. Even though Rawn knew what was happening, he had orders to wait for the arrival of Howard, and he now refused to attack or pursue the Indians until Howard arrived on the scene. Howard, however, was several days behind. Once past the entrenchments, Joseph's Indians did not stop until they had crossed the Bitter Root Valley and reached Big Hole on the border between Idaho and Montana. Here they stopped to rest, still fearing Howard's pursuit from the rear.

Meanwhile, the telegraph had once again worked its magic. General John Gibbon had been alerted and ordered from Montana with a large force of troopers to intercept the Nez Percés. Gibbon's force completely surprised Joseph and his braves in a predawn attack just a few days after the Indians had stopped to make camp at Big Hole. The camp was completely overrun and the braves scattered in all directions. As Gibbon set about burning the Indian tepees and taking women and children prisoners, Chief Joseph rallied his braves and staged a fierce counterattack. The fight that developed lasted all day and into the early evening, Gibbon finally abandoning the village and trying to form defensive positions nearby.

As soon as the camp was abandoned by the troopers, Joseph and his braves rounded up the women and children and sent them on down the trail ahead of them. Acting as a shield between the fleeing Indian families, the Nez Percé braves continued to attack the soldiers, and during the course of the life-and-death struggle in the gathering dark, General Gibbon was severely wounded. With the loss of Gibbon, the army troops also seemed to lose their spirit and retreated, taking Gibbon and their many other wounded with them.

Gibbon's forces had not retreated very far before they were reinforced by the onrushing General Howard. The combined commands now far outnumbered the Indians. But before Howard could strike with his large force of troopers and mounted infantry—in fact, on the first night the two forces were together—Chief

Joseph sent his braves on wildly dashing ponies right into the middle of the enemy camp. While there was much covering rifle fire, the Indians were not bent on inflicting casualties. What they were after was the cavalry horses, and in this effort they succeeded. The cavalry horses were herded together and under heavy cavalry guard, but the yelling braves smashed through the guard and in a few moments drove Howard's horses back down the valley into the black night. The U.S. cavalry and infantry were all foot soldiers now.

The next day Chief Joseph moved his braves and their families northeastward through Montana's rugged mountains, through Yellowstone, which had just been named a national park, and on toward Canada. Now another threat faced the Indians. The U.S. Army had sent troops to guard all of the key mountain passes. This strategy did not fool Chief Joseph, however. In fact, he warned those braves riding far out in front and acting as scouts to be alert for the first signs of the enemy.

Colonel Samuel D. Sturgis was stationed with a small body of troops at a pass on the eastern side of the uplands called Clark's Fork. Joseph's scouts warned him of the enemy's presence, but they failed to learn what a small number of troopers blocked the pass. Had Joseph been given this information, he could have easily stormed the pass and made his way on into Canada. Instead, he took a long circular detour around Clark's Fork, halting finally at a place called Canyon Creek.

It was now mid-September, and Chief Joseph and

his beleaguered band were growing weary with the constant fighting, the constant retreat. Nevertheless, at Canyon Creek they managed to fight a successful rearguard action against several hundred cavalrymen under Howard's and Sturgis's combined commands, although they lost more than a hundred ponies in the fray.

With blind determination the Nez Percés pushed on, heading now toward Montana's Bear Paw Mountains, which were just a day's ride from the Canadian border. Here, at Snake Creek, Joseph decided they would rest for the final lap of their journey. Freedom and safety were all but in sight.

At this point, Chief Joseph believed he had successfully outdistanced his pursuers. (There were some observers who later said that by a miscalculation Joseph thought he and his people had already reached Canada, but this is doubtful.) The one thing he did not reckon with was the fact that once again the telegraph had managed to outdistance him. Colonel Nelson Miles and a large force of cavalry and mounted infantry, including three troops from Custer's old Seventh Cavalry, had been alerted at Fort Keogh, Wyoming. This large command set out to cut off the Nez Percés.

Leading his men on a nonstop forced march, Miles's detachment traveled almost 300 miles in less than two weeks, hauling two field guns and several Gatling guns over extremely rough terrain. (The Gatling gun had been patented during the Civil War in 1862 by an American inventor, Dr. Richard J. Gatling. A forerunner of the machine gun, the Gatling gun was a ten-barrel, crank-operated revolving weapon that could fire between 400 and 600 rounds per minute.) They arrived at the site of Chief Joseph's camp on the wintry dawn of September 30.

Without warning, Miles's men attacked. The completely surprised Indians scattered onto a nearby ridge, and Miles's soldiers cornered them there. The Gatling guns and field guns were soon brought into play, their heavy firepower overwhelming the all-but-helpless Indians. Before surrendering, however, Joseph turned his ridge into a fortress, barricading his forces behind earthen trenches dug with knives, tomahawks and even cooking utensils. But under the heavy guns the siege could not be long withstood. Despite the hopelessness of their cause, Joseph and the last of his braves managed to hold out for several days. Then he raised a flag of truce and sent the following message to Colonel Miles:

Tell General Howard we are tired of fighting. Our chiefs are killed. The old men are all dead. My brother Ollicut who led the young braves is dead. It is cold and we have no blankets. The little children are freezing to death. Hear me, my heart is sick and sad. From where the sun now stands, I will fight no more forever.

On October 5, Chief Joseph and the remnants of his people rode into Miles's camp where General Howard was also now present. The Nez Percés had retreated more than 1,700 miles across some of the most difficult country in the West. They had fought off more than 2,000 soldiers, killing 176 of them and wounding 140 others. Joseph's force of braves had never been larger than 300, of whom 151 had been killed and 89 wounded. The survivors also included 184 squaws and 147 children, some wounded and all starving. In all, they had fought five battles. They had won three of them; one had been a standoff; and one—the last— they had lost.

Sorrowfully, Chief Joseph led his people toward the Idaho reservation. But even this last haven was to be denied them. Instead of being directed toward the reservation, they were herded into Indian Territory. There, sick and ill-fed, most of them were to die, although a few survivors were later allowed to return to their beloved Wallowa Valley. But not Joseph. He was never allowed to return to the home of his ancestors. Nevertheless, he was as good as his word. He fought no more.

With the defeat of the Nez Percés there now remained only a few pockets of Indian resistance. One of these was the homeland of the fierce Apaches in the Southwest.

10
Tigers
of the Southwest

Every year during the Indian Wars it cost the United States government more to kill an Indian than it had the year before. In 1866, for example, one estimate set the cost at $60,000 per Indian. By 1870 this figure had reached $500,000, and in the next two decades it approached the million-dollar mark. The Indians who perhaps sold their lives more dearly than any others were the fierce Apaches, whose warriors the U.S. Cavalry often called "the tigers of the Southwest." At one time there were more than 5,000 troopers in the field trying to exterminate Geronimo and his tiny band that finally dwindled to no more than thirty-six braves.

The Apaches had resisted the white man ever since the entry of the Spanish into the American Southwest in the sixteenth century. They continued their relentless war against, first, the Mexicans, and then the white Americans until late in the nineteenth century. Their war parties seldom numbered more than a hundred braves, who traveled light and killed whatever game was available for food. Often they struck murderously at one spot, vanished as quickly as they came, only to again strike a day or two later 100 or more miles away. All were past masters at ambushing unwary civilian travelers or even cavalry columns. So vicious were their attacks that the very word "Apache" was adopted as far away as Paris, France, to nickname criminal terrorists.

The Apaches had been among the first of the American Indians to acquire firearms in their early contacts with the whites. They used these weapons not only to fight the Spanish, Mexicans and white Americans but also to drive neighboring Indians from the best hunting grounds, either killing or making slaves of their captives. The Apaches were themselves threatened with enslavement when, during the American Civil War, one Arizona governor insisted that the only way to subdue them was to kill all the Apache braves and make slaves of their women and children. This policy was never carried out.

Just prior to the Civil War the Apaches had remained somewhat subdued by the presence of U.S. Army military fortresses in their territory. As these fortresses were abandoned by soldiers returning east to fight in the Civil War, the Apaches returned to the warpath, raiding white settlements and killing prospectors, miners and white settlers.

Having no high-ranking regular army officers available, the United States government called upon the legendary scout and frontiersman, Christopher "Kit" Carson, to attempt to put down the Apache uprising.

Kit Carson
PHOTO: DENVER PUBLIC LIBRARY

Commissioned a cavalry colonel, Kit Carson succeeded in subduing the Navajos, who were blood brothers of the Apaches, in 1864, but his success stopped there. After the Civil War the Apaches still reigned supreme in the Southwest.

The man selected to complete the white Americans' conquest of the Southwest was Colonel—later General—George Crook. Crook, who also later was to suffer a series of costly defeats against Chief Crazy Horse and the Sioux, had somewhat greater initial success against the Apaches. Taking command of the army in Arizona in 1871, Crook set about "saving the government millions of dollars by planning a sharp, active campaign" against the Apaches. Before Crook could mount his campaign, however, the Apaches struck in a series of fifty-four attacks throughout their territory. Led first by the Chief Victorio, then by the Chief Nana and finally by the brilliant Chief Geronimo, Apache braves were to terrorize the Southwest for the next fifteen years.

One of the first things Crook did was to recruit a small group of Apache scouts to serve as the eyes and ears of his advance cavalry units. Many Indians—especially the Pawnees—had previously served as scouts for the U.S. Cavalry, but it was not easy to obtain Apaches for this purpose. The Pawnees, like the Nez Percés, had a long tradition of friendly relations with the white man, so it was not difficult to enlist them to serve as cavalry scouts on the western plains. In fact, an entire battalion of Pawnee scouts helped protect the

Curly, a famous Indian scout

PHOTO: DENVER PUBLIC LIBRARY, WESTERN HISTORY DEPARTMENT

115

railroad construction workers while they were building the Union Pacific Railroad.

It was perhaps the successful use of Pawnee scouts that encouraged General Crook in his attempt to secure Apaches to play the same role. In addition, Kit Carson and other frontiersmen told Crook that "Only an Apache can catch an Apache." Finally, after numerous disappointments, Crook was able to hire as scouts a few Apaches who had had disagreements with their tribal leaders.

Next Crook turned his attention to the best means of transportation for the campaign of intense and relentless pursuit he planned to undertake through difficult territory and across rough terrain. The best transport, he decided, would be mules, since they could travel up to 100 miles in twenty-four hours with little or no water.

Crook supervised the selection of each mule for his campaign. He also ordered special pack saddles that would enable each mule to carry more than 300 pounds of food and ammunition. Apache country was barren country, and Crook knew that his troopers, unlike the Indians, would be unable to live off the land.

Most of Crook's mules were freighted in from Missouri. Many were young and untrained. The tails of these young, unruly mules were shaved to distinguish them from the older, steadier animals. From that time on, and especially in World War I, young, inexperienced second lieutenants just joining their army units were called Shavetails.

Crook's men were also selected with great care, and they underwent training that was every bit as rugged as that experienced by American Rangers and Green Berets in later wars. Each man was expected to survive and fight on his own if the need arose. Shoulder packs and firearms and bandoliers of ammunition weighed up to half as much as each mule carried, but no man carried an ounce of nonessential food or gear.

Crook's carefully planned winter campaign was launched in mid-November, 1872. Apache scouts spotted the first hostiles in Arizona's Salt River Canyon on the day after Christmas. Major William Brown with a detachment of Fifth Cavalry troopers was ordered to the rim of the canyon. There he discovered that the Indians were not camped on the canyon floor but in a huge cave protected by a shelf of rock halfway down the canyon wall.

Descending to a point directly opposite the cave, Brown and his men—many of whom were sharpshooters—began firing at the roof of the cave entrance. Their well-placed shots soon began to take a heavy toll of the Indians as they ricocheted off the rocky cave ceiling and went screaming into the depths of the red men's sanctuary. Soon the screams of wounded Apaches—many were women and children—matched the sound of ricocheting bullets. And then, after some hours of this murderous fusillade, another eerie sound filled the air—the Apache death chant, which meant the Indians were going to make a suicide charge.

Brown and his men, who had now been joined by reinforcements sent forward by Crook, quickly hid themselves behind rocks and boulders. When the Indians came charging out of the cave, firing on the dead run, the army riflemen picked them off with relative ease. When the Indians faltered in their charge, Brown sent some of his men up to the rim of the canyon directly over the Indians' ledge. From that vantage point the soldiers began to roll boulders down onto the hapless Apaches. Between this artificial avalanche and the relentless fire of the cavalry's rifles, the Indians' position was hopeless. Soon the few braves that were left surrendered along with their women and children. More than a hundred braves died on the rocky ledge of Salt River Canyon that day.

Colonel Crook now sent several detachments of troopers on independent sorties against the scattered bands of Apaches throughout the territory. For a time these expeditions were threatened with failure when many of the mules fell ill with fever. Trained as they were in survival tactics, however, the soldiers simply turned themselves into pack mules, carrying food and supplies on their own backs until the mules recovered.

These individual detachments met with several minor successes against the Apaches, and then Major George Randall with a battalion of infantrymen scored a major success at Turret Butte. Here a large war party was cornered atop a high plateau. With no field guns available, Randall ordered his men to scale the sheer cliff wall during the night. In a feat that would be repeated by U.S. Rangers in World War II at Point du Hoe in France on D day, June 6, 1944, the daring infantrymen painfully crawled up the cliff hand over hand and were able to launch a full-scale attack at dawn. So completely surprised were the Apaches that they were overrun almost before they could open fire. Many braves, refusing to surrender, jumped off the cliff to their deaths on the rocky canyon floor hundreds of feet below. Those who remained surrendered.

As Crook continued his campaign of constant harassment well into 1874, more and more bands of Apaches began to surrender. These men, women and children were placed on reservations, and Colonel Crook did his best to try and help them make a living as farmers. He was unsuccessful in this effort both because of the Apaches' refusal to accept a pastoral way of life and because most white Americans in the Southwest did not want Apaches living in their midst under any circumstances—they wanted them dead.

Nevertheless, Crook continued his efforts in the Apaches' behalf—building roads and irrigation ditches through the territory, installing telegraph lines, improving living conditions in every way he could. Finally, however, in 1875 Crook was promoted to brigadier general and recalled to fight the Sioux. He left behind him an apparently subdued but actually still smoldering tribe of Apache survivors. Soon they would again rise up in all their righteous wrath and strike not one but several blows against their hated white foe—blows that would be their last.

Crook had scarcely left Arizona before a group of corrupt civilian officials began to take advantage of the Apaches on their reservations. Called the Tucson

Indian Ring, this group of corrupt officials encouraged unrest among the Apaches by selling them whisky and rifles at exorbitant prices. When army officers objected to this practice, they found that the corruption spread all the way to the Indian Bureau in Washington where the contractors who were selling their services to the government were protected by federal officials. Why should the Apaches be allowed to become self-sufficient, for example, when the contractors could sell the government food for the Indians at twice or three times its worth? The Tucson Indian Ring saw to it that life on the reservations was as miserable as it could possibly be made and then encouraged the Indians to revolt. In this way the contractors who were members of the Indian Ring could make more money selling war supplies to both the government and the Indians.

The first Apaches to leave the reservation after being goaded into doing so by the Indian Ring were led by Victorio, a comparatively young chief with a genius for conducting a running fight that was similar to the genius of Chief Joseph of the Nez Percés. With no more than 100 braves Victorio led the U.S. Army on a frustrating chase for some two years through Arizona, New Mexico, Texas and back and forth across the Mexican border.

Victorio specialized in hit-and-run raids, striking quickly and unexpectedly at a white American strongpoint and then disappearing into Mexico. But the Mexicans were also determined to capture and kill the Apaches, so Victorio and his warriors actually found no peace on either side of the border. An American-

Mexican combined operation finally succeeded in trapping Victorio's war party in a canyon in Mexico where they were killed to the last man.

An ancient, rheumatic Apache chief named Nana was next to go on the warpath. From the summer of 1881 to the spring of 1882 Chief Nana and several hundred Apache braves fought more than half a dozen running battles against U.S. Army troops. He then retreated into Mexico where he joined forces with Geronimo.

Geronimo had sworn undying revenge against both the American white man and the Mexicans on the day in his youth when his mother, wife and three children had been slain by Mexicans. Little that the foe had done against him and his people since that day had made Geronimo modify his determination for vengeance. Among hard-bitten American cavalrymen Geronimo was described as "the worst Indian that ever lived." Among his own people he was a legendary hero.

Finally, near the end of 1882, the army reassigned General Crook to the Department of Arizona. Crook did his best to reorganize his constructive program for the rehabilitation of the Apaches on well-run reservations, a program that the Tucson Indian Ring had all but destroyed. The corrupt members of the Indian Ring fought Crook's reform efforts every step of the way, but he persisted. Gradually he was able to persuade many hundreds of Apaches to return to their reservations. But the one group he could not convince of his good intentions was a large party of some 500

Geronimo
PHOTO: DENVER PUBLIC LIBRARY, WESTERN HISTORY DEPARTMENT

warriors who were holding out in the rocky redoubt of Mexico's Sierra Madres. Led by Geronimo, these warriors conducted raid after raid across the border into the United States and then retreated quickly into the vastness of the Sierra Madres.

Once again Crook mounted a highly organized campaign with a task force of specially trained troops and pack trains of mules. Crook's own mule, which he rode to lead the campaign, was called Apache. In mid-1883 Crook's task force succeeded in bringing Geronimo's band to bay, and half of them surrendered. Soon afterward Geronimo also gave up the fight. Geronimo's personal surrender only took place, however, after a confrontation with General Crook, during the course of which Crook told the Apache chieftain that if he did not surrender Crook intended to hunt him down and destroy him and his remaining force if it took fifty years. Geronimo's only stipulation in surrendering was that his warriors would not be separated from their families. Crook readily agreed to this condition.

One of Crook's regulations regarding life on local reservations was that there would be no brewing or drinking of tiswin or corn beer. A few nights after Geronimo and the last of his Apaches arrived at their Arizona reservation an Indian trader smuggled not only tiswin but also the much stronger drink, mescal, which was made from fermented cactus juice, into the camp. Geronimo and some of his braves proceeded to get drunk on the bootleg alcohol and soon disappeared once again in the Sierra Madres.

When the news of another escape by Geronimo and his braves reached Washington, General Philip Sheridan relieved General Crook from duty as commander of the Department of Arizona and replaced him with General Nelson Miles.

In addition to some 5,000 men at his command—about twice as many as Crook had commanded—General Miles also had a unique signaling device. This was called a heliograph, a set of movable mirrors mounted on a tripod that was ideal for use in the clear atmosphere and bright sunlight in the high Sierra Madres. Trained operators could flash messages on a heliograph as far as thirty miles. With twenty-seven of these devices Miles was able to bracket the entire district where the Indians were hidden. In addition, he assigned highly mobile cavalry units to each area covered by a heliograph. These mobile units could go into instant action once an Indian war party was sighted and a heliograph alert was flashed across the mountain peaks.

Despite the fact that all of Miles's troops and his elaborate signaling system were concentrated on capturing Geronimo and no more than eighty Indian braves (their top strength during this period), it took almost a year and a half to trap the elusive red men. In the end it was partly because of the heliograph stations that Geronimo surrendered. Again and again he and his braves had chopped down telegraph poles and stolen the telegraph wires and thus disrupted telegraph signaling and communication efforts by the military. But there was no apparent way to stop the flashed

Morse code signals by the heliographs that alerted U.S. Army troopers to the Indians' whereabouts. To Geronimo and many of his fellow warriors there was something supernatural in these flashing mirrors that could carry news and information some 200 to 300 miles in a few relayed signals from the reflected sun.

When the relentlessly harassed Geronimo finally requested surrender terms in September, 1886, he was told they would be unconditional. Once again Geronimo stated that his only condition was that all of the Apaches now on reservations would be kept together as families. To this stipulation Miles, like Crook before him, readily agreed. But, as in the case of the Nez Percés, this agreement was never adhered to. The Apaches were first removed to Florida without any attention being paid to family memberships. Later, the Apaches were shunted from Florida to Alabama to Fort Sill in Oklahoma; finally, after a number of years, some 250 of the exiles from the Southwest were returned to New Mexico.

During the course of their forced wanderings, many of the Apaches—including the legendary Geronimo—turned at last to farming, at which they were quite successful. And in 1903 one of the most popular exhibits at the World's Fair in St. Louis was a booth at which Apache Chief Geronimo—now a successful son of the soil—was on display selling pictures of himself for a quarter apiece. But despite the fact that the aged Geronimo had apparently finally come to peace terms with the white man, he was kept under armed guard all during the fair.

11

The Massacre at Wounded Knee

*We're marching off for Sitting Bull
And this is the way we go—
Forty miles a day on beans and hay,
With the Regular Army, O!*

—OLD ARMY SONG

By a curious coincidence the last major Indian uprising in the United States occurred soon after a total eclipse of the sun. This eclipse took place on New Year's Day in 1889, and the Indians referred to it as "The Day the Sun Died."

A year earlier there had appeared in Nevada a young Paiute Indian named Wovoka, who claimed to be a messiah or a prophet. Like the Ottawa Chief Pontiac in the late eighteenth century and the Shawnee Chief Tecumseh early in the nineteenth century, Wovoka sought to unite all of the Indians into one vast federation. Unlike the warlike Pontiac and Tecumseh, however, the gentle Wovoka preached peaceful unity through the spiritual power of religion.

Shortly after the eclipse of the sun in 1889, Wovoka appeared among his people and said, "When the sun fled, I went up to Heaven and saw God and all of our people who had died a long time ago. God told me to come back and tell my people they must be good and love one another and not fight, or steal, or lie. He gave me this dance to give to my people."

Actually, the religion Wovoka preached was a blend of old Indian beliefs and Christianity's Ten Commandments. The dance he taught was called the Ghost Dance, and it was intended to prepare his people for the day they would enter paradise after a volcanic eruption occurred that would wipe out all white men and restore the old ways of Indian life. In the beginning the Ghost Dance did not incite the Indians to renewed warfare, but as its popularity spread and Wovoka's followers became more and more fanatical, the Ghost Dance took on increasingly menacing and warlike overtones. Soon the Indians began to believe that those who danced the Ghost Dance and wore special Ghost Shirts would not be harmed by white men's bullets. Finally the Ghost Dance craze and the fanatical belief in its supernatural powers spread to the Sioux reservation. There, in one of the reservation villages, sat the fierce old medicine man and chief, Sitting Bull, who had long awaited some sign or event that would give him the power to break the white man's hold over his people once and for all.

When Chief Crazy Horse had surrendered to Gen-

Sitting Bull and Buffalo Bill
PHOTO: DENVER PUBLIC LIBRARY, WESTERN HISTORY DEPARTMENT

eral Crook in the spring of 1877, he had not been accompanied by Sitting Bull, who said, "God made me an Indian but not a reservation Indian." Instead of surrendering, Sitting Bull and some of his warriors had fled to Canada, where they had remained in comparative security for several years. The only time Sitting Bull had been seriously tempted to leave his northern sanctuary was when Chief Joseph and his Nez Percés had neared the Canadian border in their epic flight from the U.S. Army. Sitting Bull's rescue efforts at that time probably would have been successful, but several of his scouts had told him that Chief Joseph and his people would be able to escape without help from the Sioux. Afterward, Sitting Bull always blamed himself for the Nez Percés' tragedy.

What finally drove Sitting Bull from Canada was famine. His followers were never large in number, and when crop failures and severe winters resulted in half of his band dying from starvation, Sitting Bull finally rode south and surrendered to American authorities in 1881. For a time he was put in prison. When he was released, he made his home in South Dakota on the Standing Rock Reservation.

Even though he was a virtual prisoner on the Standing Rock Reservation, Sitting Bull was a constant source of worry to the Indian Bureau officials and army officers. Not only was he a powerful influence, but he was still tremendously popular among all of the Indians on the reservation. In addition, he was a figure of great interest to white visitors who wanted to see "the man who killed Custer." (Actually, it had been

Crazy Horse and Gall who played the key roles in the Custer Massacre, but they had been carrying out Sitting Bull's plans.) What white officials feared was that Sitting Bull might somehow rally his Sioux braves and start another Indian uprising.

But despite these fears, Sitting Bull's fame had spread so far that he was often given permission to leave the reservation to make public appearances. One of these was at the dedication ceremonies in Bismarck to mark the completion of one more railroad, the Northern Pacific, across the continent in 1883. On this occasion Sitting Bull displayed what can only be described as a rare sense of humor. A flowery speech of congratulation to his white "brothers" had been written for Sitting Bull, who spoke fairly fluent English. But instead of reading the speech in English, Sitting Bull spoke in the Sioux language, telling the white people how much he hated them and denouncing them as thieves and liars who had stolen all of the Indian's lands. Since only one or two people present understood what the old chief was saying, the audience applauded wildly whenever Sitting Bull paused, smiled and awaited their approval. Finally, he bowed politely when he had concluded his insulting remarks, and the old chief was given a thunderous ovation.

The next summer the American government sponsored a fifteen-city tour for Sitting Bull, and this series of sold-out performances led to his being hired by Buffalo Bill Cody to take part in his popular Wild West show, or Wild West, Rocky Mountain, and Prairie Exhibition, as it was called. This show, which

Annie Oakley
PHOTO: DENVER PUBLIC LIBRARY, WESTERN HISTORY DEPARTMENT

also featured the famed trick-shot artist, Annie Oakley, played to standing-room-only crowds in both the United States and Canada. Like Geronimo, Sitting Bull also sold pictures of himself, but he usually gave away whatever money he received to the children in the audience.

At the end of their tremendously successful North American tour, Buffalo Bill told Sitting Bull he was planning on taking the show to Europe and invited the old chief to come with him. Government officials would probably have been glad to see him go, but the old chief declined.

"I am needed on the reservation," he said. "There is again talk of our lands being taken." The talk that Sitting Bull had heard was correct. Within a year the huge Sioux reservation had been split up into six small reservations with the white men keeping nine million acres for which they paid the red men $1.50 an acre. Sitting Bull did not sign the agreement to sell the land, although many other chiefs did. Afterward Sitting Bull said, "I am the only Indian left."

So Sitting Bull returned to the Standing Rock Reservation, and it was there, in 1890, that word of the new Ghost Dance religion reached him.

Some authorities claimed that Sitting Bull was preparing to take advantage of this new opportunity to rally his people for another Sioux uprising. Others claimed Sitting Bull had given his word that he would remain at peace, and he intended to keep his word. In any event, responding to rumors that the old chief was preparing to make trouble, Indian police—not soldiers—from the Standing Rock Agency moved in to arrest him on December 15. At this point Sitting Bull did give orders to his braves to resist. The result was an instant and murderous melee at close range in which Sitting Bull, six of his followers and six Indian policemen were slain.

Sitting Bull's death made immediate nationwide news. Not only as the last great symbol of Indian resistance but also as a popular showman, Sitting Bull had become a folk hero to many white Americans. A fierce controversy developed over who was responsible for his death. The dispute fanned into flames the existing disagreement between the War Department and the Interior Department's Indian Bureau regarding who was actually to blame for the continued mistreatment and killing of the Indians.

The War Department strongly objected to the fact that the army had almost no voice in Indian affairs despite the fact that it was constantly being called upon by the Indian Bureau to force Indians onto reservations, to quell reservation disturbances and to hunt down Indians who fled the reservations. This had resulted in major military efforts against the Sioux, Cheyennes, Nez Percés and Apaches. It had also caused lesser but nonetheless important campaigns against the Navajos in the Southwest and in the West against Wovoka's Paiutes, the Modocs, Bannocks and Utes.

Some 3,000 U.S. soldiers had died in 1,000 combat actions in the Indian campaigns since the Civil War, and about the same number had been wounded. Many

133

others had died from disease. While the Indians had suffered at least twice as many casualties, most army men believed that casualties on both sides could have been reduced considerably if the U.S. Army itself had a say in Indian affairs and Indian policy.

One army officer, Colonel Orlando Willcox, expressed these feelings when he testified before the U.S. Congress and said, "After depriving the Indians of their lands and proper means of subsistence, at what point in the red men's subsequent career of starvation, misery, and desperation shall you regard them as public enemies? . . . The Indian Bureau keeps feeding, clothing, and arming the Indians regardless of their behavior till they get fat and sassy, and then the army is told the Indians are troublesome and are going to war only after it is far too late to provide a remedy."

But the debate between the U.S. Army and the Indian Bureau was not yet ready to be decided. Each now blamed the other for Sitting Bull's death, a deed that the government believed threatened once again to set the western frontier aflame.

Immediately after Sitting Bull was killed his followers left their reservation villages, but they fled more in panic than in anger. Nevertheless, the army was once again charged with forcing them back onto the reservation. Custer's old regiment of troopers, the Seventh Cavalry, was given the major responsibility for rounding up the fleeing Indians, and within two weeks had largely succeeded in accomplishing its mission. But General Nelson Miles was not satisfied with the fact that one renegade red man, Chief Big Foot, was still at large.

Big Foot was in charge of a force of some 350 Indians, about half of whom were women and children. On December 28, four troops of Seventh Cavalry intercepted Big Foot's band, who claimed they were riding in to give themselves up at South Dakota's Pine Ridge Agency. The cavalrymen said they would escort the Indians to the agency, and the red men agreed. That night the Sioux and their soldier escort camped at a place called Wounded Knee Creek. Before dawn the military escort was joined by the rest of the Seventh Cavalry under the command of Colonel James Forsyth. Forsyth had orders from Miles to disarm the Indians and take them to a railhead in nearby Nebraska for shipment to Omaha.

The Sioux awakened on the morning of December 29, 1890, to find themselves completely surrounded by more than 500 cavalrymen. Also staring down on the Indian encampment were several small cannons called Hotchkiss guns. The troopers now moved in to disarm the warriors, but an argument resulted when the Indians refused to give up their Winchester repeating rifles. They had been urged not to give up their weapons by a Ghost Dancing medicine man named Yellow Bird. Yellow Bird told the Sioux braves that if they gave up their guns they would be killed. He also insisted that if they kept their guns and wore their Ghost Shirts, no bullets from the white men's weapons could harm them. The braves responded by trying to conceal their repeating rifles under their blankets.

The troopers now began to use force to seize the red men's guns, and in one scuffle between a trooper and an Indian brave a single rifle shot was fired. Instantly there were volleys fired by both sides, and a long and terrible melee resulted, with Indians and soldiers fighting hand to hand. As the Indians gradually began to scatter, the soldiers backed out of the village, and then the Hotchkiss guns were brought into play. These devastating weapons were aimed mainly at the tepees in which women and children were trying to hide. The chaos created by this close range cannonade lasted only a few murderous minutes. When it had ended, more than 150 Indians, 62 of them women and children, lay dead or dying. Included in the slain were Chief Big Foot and the Ghost Dancer, Yellow Bird. Fifty other Indians were wounded. The cavalrymen had lost 25 killed and 39 wounded.

The Seventh Cavalry had avenged Custer's defeat.

Wounded Knee was the last major battle between Indians and the white man within the continental United States. Wovoka took off his Ghost Shirt and, in Indian mourning custom, placed a blanket over his head, urging his people to follow the white man's way of life. Within a few short weeks the Ghost Dance movement was over—and so were the Indian Wars, or almost. For in a very real sense the Indian Wars and their terrible aftermath are still with us today.

As recently as the mid-1970s, members of the American Indian Movement continued to demand that the United States government live up to the hundreds of treaties it made—and broke—with the Indians years ago. In an attempt to end the continued exploitation of the "native Americans," Indians briefly seized the headquarters of the Bureau of Indian Affairs in Washington, staged a seventy-one-day armed occupation of Wounded Knee, and danced the Ghost Dance on the South Dakota Sioux Reservation. The Ghost Dance once again failed to protect the demonstrators from physical harm, and there were bloody clashes with white police. Nor did it seem able to protect the sons of the plains Indians any more than it had their fathers from the white man's laws. Many of the demonstrators—as well as the lawyers who defended them—were arrested and sent to jail.

Bibliography

American Heritage editors, *The Confident Years*, American Heritage, New York, 1969.

———, *Book of Indians*, American Heritage, New York, 1961.

Berky, Andrew S. and Shenton, James P., *The Historians' History of the United States*, G. P. Putnam's Sons, New York, 1966.

Brown, Dee, *Bury My Heart at Wounded Knee*, Holt, Rinehart and Winston, Inc., New York, 1971.

———, "The Settlement of the Great Plains," *American History Illustrated*, June 1974.

Custer, General George A., *My Life on the Plains*, R. R. Donnelley & Sons Company, Chicago, 1952.

Deloria, Vine, Jr., "Centuries of Struggle Between Indians and Whites," *Compton's Encyclopedia*, Chicago, 1974.

Downey, Fairfax, *Indian-Fighting Army*, Charles Scribner's Sons, New York, 1941.

Finerty, John H., *War-Path and Bivouac*, R. R. Donnelley & Sons Company, Chicago, 1955.

Gabriel, Ralph Henry, editor, *The Pageant of America*, Yale University Press, New Haven, 1929.

Grinnell, George Bird, *Two Great Scouts and Their Pawnee Battalion*, University of Nebraska Press, Lincoln, 1928, 1973.

Hagan, William T., *American Indians*, University of Chicago Press, Chicago, 1961.

Leckie, Robert, *The Wars of America*, Harper & Row, New York, 1968.

Leckie, William H., *The Buffalo Soldiers*, University of Oklahoma Press, Norman, 1967, 1970.

McConkey, Harriet E. Bishop, *Dakota War Whoop*, R. R. Donnelley & Sons Company, New York, 1965.

McNickle, D'Arcy, "North American Indians," *Encyclopaedia Britannica*, 1973.

Marshall, Brigadier General S. L. A. Custer, "The Little Big Decisions," *Army* magazine, June 1971.

Momaday, Natachee, "American Indians," *American Educator Encyclopedia*, 1974.

Paladin, Vivian A., editor, "The Joseph Myth," *The Magazine of Western History*, Winter 1972.

Prucha, Francis Paul, *The Sword of the Republic*, The Macmillan Company, New York, 1969.

Rickey, Don, Jr., *Forty Miles a Day on Beans and Hay*, University of Oklahoma Press, Norman, 1963, 1972.

Ruppel, Maxine, *White Buffalo's Story*, Montana Reading Publications, 1970.

Schott, Joseph L., *Above and Beyond*, G. P. Putnam's Sons, New York, 1963.

Tebbell, John, *The Compact History of the Indian Wars*, Hawthorn Books, Inc., New York, 1966.

Terrell, John Upton, *American Indian Almanac*, Thomas Y. Crowell Company, New York, 1971.

———, and Walton, Colonel George, *Faint the Trumpet Sounds*, David McKay Company, Inc., New York, 1966.

Trobriand, Phillippe de, *Army Life in Dakota*, R. R. Donnelley & Sons Company, Chicago, 1941.

Utley, Robert M., *Frontier Regulars*, The Macmillan Company, New York, 1973.

———, *Frontiersmen in Blue*, The Macmillan Company, New York, 1967, 1973.

Weigley, Russell F., *History of the United States Army*, The Macmillan Company, New York, 1967.

Index

141

Gatling gun, 108–9
Geronimo, 74, 100, 111, 114, 132; and Apache's last stand, 121, 123–25
Gettysburg, 66
Ghost Dance, 127, 132, 135, 136, 137
Gibbon, Gen. John, 106
Grant, Ulysses S., 68, 92, 103
Grummond, Lt. George W., 3

Harrigan and Hart (vaudeville team), 53
Harrison, Gen. William Henry, 18
Hayfield Fight, 29–30, 35
Heliograph, 124–25
Homestead Act of 1862, 42
Hotchkiss guns, 135–36
Howard, Gen. Oliver O., 103–4, 105, 106, 107, 108, 109

Immigrants, in U.S. Army, 53–54
Indian Removal Act, 18–19
Indian Territory, 18, 19, 21, 23
Indians. *See* American Indian(s), *also individual tribes*
Iroquois Indians, 17

Jackson, Andrew, 19, 68
Jefferson, Thomas, 41
Jenness, Lt. John, 31, 34
Joseph, Chief, 21, 74, 100, 103–10, 120, 129

Kentucky Red (horse), 8 ff.
Keogh, Capt. Myles W., 69, 83–84, 93, 96
King Philip's War, 16

Kiowa Indians, 71, 75; Red River War, 76, 77, 79, 80, 81, 82

Lee, Gen. Robert E., 66, 68
Lewis, Meriwether, 100, 101
Lincoln, Abraham, 25, 40
Little Bighorn, Custer's last stand at, 65, 69, 82, 91, 92–96, 100
Little Crow, Chief, 25

Mackenzie, Col. Ranald, 79, 80
McClellan, Gen. George, 83
"Manifest destiny," 41–42
Massasoit, 16
Miles, Col. Nelson, 77, 79, 99, 108–9, 124, 134
Modoc Indians, 133
Mohawk Indians, 17

Nana, Chief, 114, 121
Navajo Indians, 114, 133
New Ulm, 25
Nez Percé Indians, 21, 74, 114, 120, 125, 129, 133; last stand of, 100–10

Oakley, Annie, 132
Ollicut, 109
Oregon Territory, 21
O'Sullivan, John L., 42

Paiute Indians, 133
Palo Duro Canyon, 80
Pawnee Indian scouts, 114, 116
Pequot Indians, 14, 16
Philip, 16